THE
MAGIC
FORMULA

The importance on staff engagement on
transforming a business into success

DAVID CRABB

Cover design by SpiffingCovers.com

SECTIONS IN THIS BOOK

ABOUT THE AUTHOR

David qualified as a Polymer Chemist, rubbed shoulders with those far more qualified, and had no end of chemical experiments go wrong. Some caught fire, with some colleagues and himself sustaining injuries, thankfully just minor family abrasions. After one or two damaged pieces of expensive laboratory equipment, he decided to take a promotion into the commercial world, away from chemicals, experiments and immediate danger (to those around him, that is).

After a fast track training programme, he stayed content in the commercial world, leaving behind this trail of destruction. Suddenly, he was free to let loose on clients, suppliers and businesses, making a career out of chemistry in the business world.

One thing is certain, mistakes can be good, providing no one was injured along the way. Learnings from these mistakes can be applied to future learnings, and to improve one's skills, knowledge and abilities.

As a Leader, David has been in the *Sunday Times* Top 100 Companies to work for several times. He is passionate about people engagement, building teams and helping people succeed in their careers.

David thrives on business challenges, favouring companies that are in need of a positive turnaround, a particular fix or organisational transformation.

The book was written after David sold a Company in December 2016, having led its turnaround from disaster to success. In this book, David hopes to share some of his experiences with others, adding a little light entertainment along the way through his own style of storytelling.

This chapter of life follows several other business turnarounds, resulting in a culmination of experiences and knowledge. In the pages that follow, David has pieced together some common threads, things he observed and experienced throughout each turnaround, and knitted these together to form a colourful and interwoven pattern of short sections designed to be bite-sized, digestible chunks of meaty experience to nourish the brain, provoke thought and stimulate ideas.

THANK YOU FROM THE AUTHOR

The book is dedicated to Thomas and Alice, my two younger children, who keep me young at heart, poor of pocket and thankful for choosing to have a good work-life balance, which I put right after recovering from meningitis in 2010.

This book is about business, making business a success and the challenges that this presents along the way.

It is written in the hope of helping managers move into effective and successful Leadership roles, which can be both a tough and rewarding journey.

Thank you for choosing to read this. I hope you love it, share it, learn from it and, possibly, relate to it.

Enjoy

SO, WHAT'S YOUR STRATEGY?

'So, what's your strategy?' I have lost count of the number of times people have asked this question when they realised I had turned around and helped several businesses.

My glib response, even in an interview, appears a little arrogant, 'What do you mean?' In return, they ask, 'You know, what's the key to your success? The one thing that made it happen.'

During the interview, not surprisingly, I was expecting the uneducated question, the interviewer looking for the opportunity to shortcut years of experience with a silver bullet of a response. I am incredulous that they truly believe that turning a business from failure to success is reliant on one aspect alone. The

11

confidence in the question, suggesting that success is quick or easy, is almost offensive.

Can it be that easy? Can one create a fast turnaround in the case of a broken or damaged business? Or must it be complex and verging on the impossible? Thankfully, I have done this, so it cannot be impossible. But, I can honestly state that it is never easy.

Nor is it dependent on myself alone. This requires team effort, everyone pulling together and working towards the same goal. Making sure the team works well together is ultra-important.

Essentially, anyone seeking a one phrase answer will be disappointed. So, what was my response?

Well, imagine the interviewer getting more than they expected during the meeting. A one phrase answer is possible, but it would not be a polite one.

I do not wish to appear rude to anyone. As with life, a business is complex. A question needs to generate a wider response, and give it the space it deserves.

My answer can be explained in a variety of ways: relayed via my own stories and through my experiences based on real events, quotes and interactions with people, some of whom are far more intelligent than I could ever hope to be. I will break this down in the pages that follow.

THE MAGIC FORMULA

Business challenges fall into similar categories, which are usually specific to the business in question, regardless of its industry. Rarely does the opportunity arise where one can simply copy and paste exact strategies from one business to another. Recently, someone asked, 'You must have a template to put in place by now? Like a recipe, something the next person can copy and replicate to get a guaranteed outcome.' 'Ah, like a cake mix with instructions?' I returned.

As a qualified research chemist, repetition of basic processes is something I am quite familiar with, adopting minor variances along the way to achieve the desired outcome. Creating a business turnaround template is not quite the same thing, and it is not an easy task. If it were, surely someone far more enterprising than myself would have patented it by now, and retired early with the respect of thousands of fans, along with the admiration and lifelong friendship of their wealth adviser.

In my IT business, one of the core messages to our clients is that, regardless of size, sector or geographic location, businesses face similar challenges. These types of challenges can be overcome with technical solutions, which has proven to be the case.

Every business, however similar on the surface, is unique. Its turnaround journey will differ from the next. However, there is a major variable, one that cannot be predicted in finite terms. Something integral but often ignored in the aspect of business turnaround: its people.

Every section in this book will focus on people in some form or another. I make no excuses for this overlap, repetition or predictability.

So, no shock announcements. In the sections that follow, there will be a strong emphasis on the importance of people as it is these people who represent the biggest variable and highest common denominator, combined.

I typically liken a Company to the shape of a hand … please don't be alarmed, put the book back or ask for a refund just yet! … The five digits represent five typical functions, and the palm represents the people who hold everything together, without which the functions could not exist.

The role of the Leader is often misinterpreted, with most Leaders operating as specialists in one of the five main functional areas, rather than specialising in Leadership itself. In reality, this is a role that requires its own focus, as we will go on to explore.

The Leader is responsible for pulling all the functions together, revolving around the people who make the function happen. However, not everyone is perfectly suited to their function. This Leadership responsibility alone is a skill in itself. A skill that can be learnt. Although, being passionate about staff engagement is something that must be felt, believed in and practiced every day. It is not something that can be taught. I look forward to explaining this further as we go along, in my own strange, quirky style, and through real life stories.

THE ROLE OF THE LEADER

The Leadership role is repeatedly misunderstood, and its function vague. I often hear people confuse the word 'Leadership' with management. I say 'confuse' as I do not believe that this is intentional, just apathetic.

The Leader, in the case of business transformation, takes on many forms of responsibility. This requires a high degree of flexibility and adaptability in order to meet necessary business changes, whilst retaining the core vision throughout.

During the initial stage of transforming a business, it is sometimes necessary for a Leader to take immediate and direct action. Although I favour democracy among the team, critical actions do surface, ones that cannot be delegated easily, or delayed in favour of a healthy debate.

I associate this inherent requirement with a fire-fighter who sees a building on fire. The fire-fighter kicks in the door, runs up the stairs and drags out endangered people. They do not have the time to meet, discuss, agree and determine an action plan. Anyone who knocks on a door and waits for permission to enter, might just be too late to save the day.

Thankfully, in the world of business transformations, such extreme action is rare. Although, the impact of delaying in the event of an extreme situation, where immediate action is required, could result in a business going bust. In my experience, I have witnessed this happen on a few occasions, causing the Company to withdraw from purchases, terminate client contracts, close offices, obtain financial support and make redundancies. The ability to maintain a Company's trading is dependent on speedy decision-making and change, with no time for apologies or debates.

The Leader could equate themselves to a chameleon. They play the role of a pace setter, a person who can adapt and react to emergencies, then revert, with ease, to the democratic way of leading others to the cause. I strongly believe this is the right approach when such circumstances arise.

A manager, on the other hand, should be adept at managing the finer detail of transactions, a constant force delivered consistently until the pace is changed by the Leader. Steady people management skills are essential, particularly when the people themselves can be extremely inconsistent. The skill set required of a manager to keep the pace flowing should never be understated. Leaders simply cannot do their jobs unless the managers are performing well.

Equally, the Leader must also be able to manage, an indispensable skill, somewhat. Although, in the case of transforming businesses, it is not a long-term deployment.

To clarify, a Leader who delivers transformation and thrives on change, will need a major end point, or milestone. Conversely, the manager's approach to managing people and processes remains constant, with outputs as their end points.

What happens when the Leader reaches their end point and delivers? Naturally, that depends on the end point. From my perspective, the end point is when the Company is performing better and the rest of the Leadership Team/board is self-sufficient and capable of doing their jobs without constant evaluation or support from the Leader, working together smoothly towards the same objective.

My personal style is to ensure a short-term succession plan is reached. Following the implementation of radical changes, it is essential to coach or evolve others into managing the Company during the phase of stability.

So, what happens to the Leader, as in my case?

I always attempt to make myself redundant. By this, I do not mean I must leave, never to darken their door again. Of course, however, that is an option, one seriously worth considering if you like change.

In essence, by empowering the team to run the day-to-day business and become self-sufficient, the Leader can focus on longer term growth and other things, such as M&A activity.

I refer to this as the NOW & NEXT. With 'now' being the day-to-day, and 'next' being just that.

A Company that is reliant on growth requires someone to champion the 'next', someone who has the time and the ability to focus on this without compromising the Company's day-to-day activities.

This thought process, however, is exceptionally difficult for many Leaders. To achieve this mindset, Leaders often detach themselves through making their previous roles redundant. This detachment brings with it its own insecurities, especially when Shareholders view an opportunity to create savings in the form of your salary and costs.

We will explore this in more depth later on. But, for now, let me leave you with this thought …

Making yourself redundant means you have done a great job of empowering, coaching and developing your team, creating next Leaders. If you do not create space for yourself to Lead the next big thing … who will?

LAYING THE FOUNDATIONS

Having formed many Leadership Teams in different industries, I recognise that people must be empowered to take charge. Give them accountability and, those who can, will thrive on it.

For this to be successful, the Leader must be prepared to transfer responsibilities on to other people — scary stuff!

Recently, someone I was coaching asked me how I let go. Well, now, that's a tricky one, and it often goes wrong.

Further on, we touch on building and forming a team and creating a mixture of complementary skills. The intention behind building on people's skills is to form a foundation that encourages active support among team members, not just in the sense of being nice and friendly, but in the form of challenging their thinking and being controversial at times, whilst respecting one another enough to know when to yield to the other person's expertise.

It is imperative the Leader focuses on this, the formation of a team that can get on without them. It is crucial that individuals are confident enough to lean on one another for support (in many forms), and get by, regardless of the circumstances, and without the Leader.

Perhaps this is the scary part ... the recruitment of people who do not rely on you every minute of the day. The perspective of intimidation stems from the Leader struggling to find direction.

I recall a friend, a CEO of a large Company, commenting on his job. It was his first CEO role, having already held numerous high profile Directorship positions. He once told me that, after resolving a few initial challenges, such as setting the Company on the right path and putting a great team in place, he ended up with a rather proficient team, leaving him with little to do.

Not wishing to be flippant, he was, of course, highly skilled and never let an hour go by without being active within his business. His effectiveness in dealing with the initial challenges led to a decline in Leadership specific tasks.

This is a crucial point for any Leader. Where one avoids the temptation of feeding their own appetite for being hands on within a function, migrating at a stressful time towards things they love or are particularly good at. This works fine in small businesses, where there is no functional Director fulfilling each individual function or role. But imagine how painful it would be for all when the Leader suddenly starts doing the job of the Operations Director (for example).

This meddling is not healthy, not productive or respectful to the team. It has the potential to create a huge wedge between the Leader and their Leadership Team, even to the point of frustration, unhappiness and resignation of your team. Ideally, without the need for violent outbursts and pistols at dawn.

The Leader must respect and trust the Leadership Team to act, daily, in their respective functions. Otherwise, why the hell did you hire them?

The role of the Leader at this point (in regard to the team), is to make an impact on them in a different way, to coach and to guide them on their path and help them deal with their daily challenges like a chief adviser. In return, the Leader gathers all the detailed information they need, without having to demand a printed report.

Senior staff do not want their toes trod on. They need our support and encouragement to go from good to great with help from a Leader, help that is not always given praise or recognition. Hence, the role of the Leader can be a lonely one, indeed. It is not just about friendships, otherwise we would all bring our dogs to meetings, but the isolation one can feel when not praised in proportion to effort, can be difficult to handle.

Being chief adviser allows a degree of independence and detachment from the level of detail the Leadership Team is caught up in, and the objectivity that is desperately needed. At the same time, they can influence the direction of delivery through simple remarks such as, 'Did I come up with that, or did you?', as a great way of leaving a discussion that generates a new idea. Getting there together empowers the team member whilst allowing the Leader to influence the direction. Yet, the buy in and acceptance will be huge by comparison.

So, how do you form a team that works?

Given my points above, it is fairly clear that a Leader needs people who know their stuff. So, do you go for industry veterans, or passionate people who thrive on making an impact?

Ideally, you need both. Of course, finding this mix is not always easy. Occasionally, hiring a competitor almost always involves baggage being brought with them, which may be counter-intuitive.

I like to think that passion in making a difference is the most important ingredient, if I needed to choose. Knowledge can be taught, passion cannot.

Obviously, I refer to those with talent and passion, not just angry politicians looking to preach anti-establishment crap to undermine everyone other than themselves. I hope you see where I am coming from?

I would, however, purposefully bring in the outspoken one (I will cover this in more detail later), to add a little controversial argument and keep any negativity as close as possible. This strategy helps the Leader challenge their own decision-making and thinking, as it sheds light on what others may be thinking. So, how do you get the complementary skills?

Experience provides the best platform for judging this. Although, Psychometric profiling tools also support the process with a much-needed boost.

Some of you may be thinking that this is a load of old rubbish, that these tools are not all they are cracked up to be. If you are in any doubt, get an HR professional (registered in using these) to perform one on yourself.

I recall, many years ago, going for a Sales Manager role with my, then, employer, a huge Company and industry leader throughout the world. It was an opportunity for promotion. I was told I would not get the job immediately (as they were a bunch of self-proclaimed snobs), although the experience would be good for me, apparently (condescending twats!).

The Psychometric profile was shared with me. Yet, my youthful arrogance failed to accept that the feedback was really for me. Other than recognising the name at the top, I think someone had switched the profiles purposefully, as if MI5 operated in HR (it could, of course).

Reading the profile many years later, I had no choice but to recognise and accept the points the profile highlighted to me at the time, well … it was me, really, with not a saboteur in sight.

I have kept this profile from 1989; it serves as a reminder that these tools (that have advanced significantly over the last three decades) are an accurate insight into a person's preferences, character traits and how they perform under stress.

Taking this a step further, I recall an interview where a business owner asked me where I intended to get my Leadership Team from. My response shocked him. He had been under the impression I was going to hire the big guns at a big cost to build a Leadership Team. It was a sneaky question, I think, as he was ready to shoot me down for spending his hard-earned green stuff on recruitment fees and big salaries.

Naturally, I announced that, by performing internal profiling exercises, you could typically unveil the skills you needed. Although, this would depend on the scale of challenges. I find it amazing that companies who employ staff, fail to recognise the enormity of skills staring back at them every day. Their ambitions are put in boxes by the very management who employ them, squashing, squeezing and containing every ounce of aspiration they have. Our job as Leaders, in this context, is to recognise their talent and workout how we can put it to great use.

Just imagine the fun and motivation to be had in identifying and developing your own talent from within your own Company.

Well, every Company does this to some extent, although it takes a little time to analyse why people leave. This is a seriously good investment, with a direct impact on Leadership time as, sometimes, team managers tell you what they want you to hear, thereby preserving their own failings (human nature, of course).

Money is not always the biggest factor. I will cover this in greater depth further on as it is important.

Giving people the chance to shine will engage them. It is true that not everyone gets there, but I would rather lose staff after recognising their limitations, having given them the chance, rather than judging their capabilities based on what they have not done (yet), or because they are particularly successful in their current role.

Another Director once challenged my decision to promote a person to Marketing Manager. This person had been appointed by their predecessor to the role of Marketing Assistant. From the Director's perspective, the person would remain an assistant. As tough as it sounds, it is a common decision people make.

It is important to recognise that most managers are not born into their roles, they evolve like us all, thank goodness. Otherwise, I would always be seen as someone in nappies, unable to feed myself (yes, I know, I am heading back to that point with the coming years of old age!).

After getting to know the Marketing Assistant, I recognised, quite easily, just how knowledgeable, passionate and enthusiastic they were. They would be just as capable of doing the job, possibly as well as any other external candidate. Yet, this person had been kept in the shadows for some time, the shadow of their previous manager, by simply respecting reporting lines, being loyal to a fault and, yes, you guessed it, being completely overlooked.

I have the view that everyone has a talent. Our job as Leaders is to discover it, use it and develop it.

Yet, it is not the easy option, it is the harder option. It is easier for a Leader to inform their Shareholders that they have recruited an external applicant. Recruiting from a competitor is something Shareholders love as they feel they have the potential to gain some insight into a competitor's success whilst getting one over on the competition (completely understandable). Recruiting internally can create two problems: backfilling and nurturing.

Whilst hiring externally, which is essential at times, can bring greatness from another Company, there are no guarantees that this approach works, that your culture works for them, or that they will even stay.

Promoting from within, will, if you get it right, create a culture of investment in people (not just saying it – doing it). Forming and maintaining loyalty both ways can make an impact just as quickly as an external hire.

After forming a great and successful Leadership Team in my Software business, we were in preparation for sale, where I and a few others would depart as Shareholders. We decided to form a new Operations Board that would help strengthen the Company at a tactical level. The team members were already in situ as managers, so the focus was on making it click, rather than bringing a bunch of new people together.

Using the Psychometric profiling I referred to earlier, we recruited people as managers, so we knew what we had to work with already.

Let's remember that there is no right and wrong when it comes to these things. The Leader's decisions can only be as good as the information they have. This information is necessary for Leaders to understand how to get the best from managers, and for others to understand why they behave as they do.

The Operations Board members were experienced, they knew their jobs and could take responsibility for their own functions. This was no different from my previous experiences. Yet, for some reason, the members were not clicking as well as the Leadership Team I'd formed – why?

Just from attending meetings with them, it was clear they were just not clicking. Okay, they got on well and were given topics to discuss, which they helped form decisions on. So, what was missing?

They were brought together to represent the whole business. This meant that they were there because of their functions, rather than through desire. When I say this, I mean they were passionate Leaders, there out of a desire for status, which was certainly not in short supply.

It was a lesson I'd taken from the 'Weakest Link' television programme (and my section on this in the book).

I'd created a sense of insecurity, an insecurity that revolved around this new Operations Board forming the team, not me.

It was known that, after some months, we would refine the team structure to one they chose, one that complemented themselves and their skills, a team that fulfilled a value in each meeting and every day in between. The team of 15 would potentially diminish in size.

The weak would not survive; the strong would be rewarded through peer recognition, and financially.

And so, we began. Each person on the Operations Board was given three votes. The members voted for each other based on their views on how the other contributed to the meetings, as well as in-between meetings.

Three points were given to first place, then two points and one point respectively, with reasoning.

Each month, they would vote anonymously. I collated these and awarded a share of the bonus pot, £1,500 per month, to be shared proportionately between the top five scores.

If one didn't receive a bonus, they were not in the top five that month, and were expected to try harder. The threat was not a reduction in pay or of losing their jobs, but the removal of status … ah, now I got it, they feared loss.

Only three months into this, which was much quicker than I had imagined, the delineation was obvious.

Ten people were receiving a good spread of votes based on their perceived contribution; the other five hardly received any.

I loved not being the bad guy (for a change), and that their removal from the Operations Board came as no surprise when the news was delivered.

Their removal, however, was not taken as a matter of fact. They continued to fight back for their position on the Operations Board, clambering to convince their colleagues of their achievements each month, which was good for keeping the bar high.

And so, the Operations Board made decisions themselves, as a committee, without autocratic thinking. A decision based purely on perceived contributions, interaction and value the member brought to the wider team.

Through this, a team had been created. They had been rewarded along the way, but more importantly, they had been empowered to make decisions, important decisions previously reserved for Directors only.

Interestingly, over the course of time, further delineation was observed … and the discovery of our next Director. Who knew!

His recognition came as no shock. Everyone was pleased. It also showed the development path for themselves through this announcement.

LEAVE YOUR PROBLEMS AT HOME

Early on in my career, I was on my way to visit a potential client, a large international business. It was the type of client we wanted, the sort of client that shouted out to other clients as a reference. They were the Holy Grail of contracts, attracting all kinds of sales people.

The meeting, understandably, was a very important one. As I was a relative newcomer to my career and my employer, the MD accompanied me. The MD for heaven sake! What great exposure! I was getting noticed; today was the start of something exciting, and nothing was going to spoil it. My route was planned and I'd factored in plenty of time to get there. My preparation was done and I was on top form. Not arrogant, but confident. We did, after all, have a great story to tell and the opportunity to sell this to a Board who needed what we had to offer.

My conversation with the Managing Director was going well. We were getting on and he seemed genuinely interested. Although, I suspected that this was just the gregarious credentials of a Leader at work, so I maintained my professional guard. In one of my previous roles, there was a Director who would attend the Christmas party behaving like he was merry on the fizz. We only later realised that he never touched a drop. He used this guise to get close to people, to find out what they really thought, before striking like a snake on the heathland, lashing out when the time was right, based on his newfound information. The Director seemed to use this as his strategic weapon, surgically removing his problems from his landscape. No! I must not give too much away. Keep it calm, David, professional. Nothing was getting through my social firewall.

Then it happened.

Following some recent good results, I was given a new car. It was fitted with the latest technology, a car telephone. Well, it was the 80s and such things were not commonly available. As it was new, a ringing phone on full volume was hard to ignore. It was a call. I wondered who could be calling and my heart started racing. I wasn't sure what to do. Should I just ignore it? My MD looked at me and stated, 'Well, it might be important ...' He must have been right as only a few people had my number.

The moment I answered, I was filled with regret. My hands-free conversation with my, then, wife (and no I did not divorce her for this) flowed like any natural conversation between a husband and wife (okay, get your minds out of the gutter. We had young children!). 'The washing machine has broken,' she said. I was desperate to get her off the line so I calmly told her I would call her back in a couple of hours. Well, this turned out to be a rather ill-fated situation. Hands-free conversations often only went one way at a time, and she was not pausing for breath. From her perspective, with two young children, no money and no clean clothes, disaster had struck.

My wife continued to remind me of our credit card position. In other words, she shared the fact that we could not afford to buy a new washing machine, even on our maxed-out cards. Joy! Any hope of leaving my problems at home were now just a pipe dream.

I was, and still am, a proud man. Needless to say, I felt embarrassed by the fact my new employer was now aware of the cracks upon my strong, confident shell. My standing was being diminished by each passing second. Two thoughts rushed through my head: firstly, how to stop her talking? And, secondly, how would I pay for a new washing machine?

Thankfully, the call ended soon after. I apologised to my MD, whereby he calmly asked his flustered driver to pull over into a lay-by.

This is it, I thought, I am going to get a bollocking. Then again, it was nothing more than I deserved. A perfect day derailed.

I carried on driving until he sternly asked me to pull over, which I did.

He wanted to talk to me about my problem, but I was not accessible. I had shut down, I was embarrassed. I was certainly not the same, confident man he had started the journey with.

Eventually, he managed to extract the cost of a new washing machine from me. I gave the figure of £400 (typical man. I had no idea 30 years ago!). Using my phone, he called our head office.

He instructed the Finance Director (FD) to arrange for a net bonus of £400 to be paid into my account that very day. Then, on his instructions, I called my wife back and proudly told her what had happened. But, I used the handset this time!

Later, my MD told me that he was quite pleased that the call had come through while we were driving, rather than before I left home for work that day. It had given him the opportunity to remove an otherwise unknown problem. His motives were simple. Having sorted the problem that would have played on my mind, he ensured my focus was on the objective we had that day. I was free from external pressures and worries, and better able to focus on my performance.

From that day forward, I have adopted the same view. If I can help remove an external worry, financial or otherwise, my team stay focused on the business objectives. Although, a Leader who is genuinely interested in their role is also needed to maintain the team's focus.

Similarly, there is little point in insisting a person remains at their desk until 5 p.m. if you know they need to be elsewhere. It is unlikely for them to contribute anything good or productive. Also, they're more likely to go off sick, resulting in their commitment being noticeably diminished.

Understanding your team's pressures and motivations will take time, genuine interest and sincerity. But, pay attention to the logic here. Performance at work is often affected by personal or external factors. Rather than pushing the employee for results, find ways to get the best from your people, instead. This is likely to result in the retention of an employee, one who is committed to doing a great job.

LET'S GET ENGAGED

Staff engagement is a key theme that forms the platform throughout this book, although not always referred to as the title suggests.

A recruiter recently asked me what I do professionally. My response was: 'I am a business Leader. I am a CEO/MD.'

Although this was clearly stated in my CV, they continued with their questioning: 'Which department do you work in? Sales, HR, or finance, perhaps?'

'Yes,' I said, barely managing a sense of respect and holding back my annoyance.

'So, which is it?' they immediately persevered, tersely.

'Leadership and people,' I responded.

'Okay. So HR then,' came the ignorant clarification.

I am certain I will not be on their Christmas card mailing list as my next response was rather vicious. Did they genuinely not recognise Leadership as a talent, a job in its own right? This was an executive Search Company. In my humble opinion, this recruiter should have been shot at dawn (or any other time for that matter). He needed to be refrained from sounding and acting like an idiot. I really am not a violent person, I must add. However, after my outburst, I proceeded to explain what I meant, and offered more depth to my previous response.

He seemed confused with the concept of Leadership and management. By this point in the interview, I was in no mood to help educate him. Perhaps, if I had a loaded gun, I may have welcomed him to the class!

Eager to move on, I diverted the line of discussion to focus on what I meant by staff engagement. He took this shift optimistically and even went on to talk positively on the matter. It did make him sound like an expert on the subject, somewhat. Finally, I thought, we're getting somewhere. We have a common language between us, and a topic we could talk sensibly about.

He then went on to tell me that his Company was great at staff engagement. It was common practice for his Directors to provide daily instructions to the team and refresh their targets. In doing so, they felt that they had engagement with the Board. Oh dear! The credibility brakes were on again. What a complete Muppet! This chap was in no position to place an executive, ever. Although, I guess, lady luck helps all of us at some point, somehow. So, even he might have stood a chance.

What's interesting is the fact that the phrase 'staff engagement' is not always understood, and may register differently with different people.

Who really gets it, then? I was proud to enter two Companies I had been a part of for the *Sunday Times* Top 100 Companies to Work For awards, run by 'Best Companies', recognising that Leadership is about creating a culture that people want to work in. I am not saying that you need to give people three hours a day off to do Pilates and play the Xbox, but a culture where staff feel valued, where their ideas are heard, where there is a clear goal, and, more importantly, why they continue to do it.

A place where hard work is recognised, where communications are opened up to prevent the need for rumours to circulate, just the spreading of facts.

I admit that, being open and honest to all staff members can be a scary thing for both Leaders and some staff. Although a Company may operate an open-door policy, where people welcome the truth and complete openness, this can be rather daunting for some. So, it is not for everyone. However, there is the potential to create a culture by recruiting staff that seek this culture. I have been amazed by the number of people I have encountered who hate their working culture because they are not allowed to express themselves, have restricted input, are not heard or are not taken seriously. Such people (and there are loads of them) would seek an environment that provides such an open culture, where there is greater transparency, allowing them to be in the know about every day happenings, whilst being aware of the difference their contribution makes.

I recently met a CEO, one who was very proud of his business, as CEO's typically are ...

We were at an event and absorbed in a discussion on staff engagement and its importance.

We certainly shared similar views on its importance, but I am not sure we were in alignment on the path towards achieving this. So, I was keen to listen and happy to learn from him.

He mentioned the provision of a room with a pool table, SKY TV and games console, comfy chairs and a CD player, as well as space to eat their lunch. Ultimately, his team worked long hours because of this.

In return, I told him a little about how I approach staff engagement. I mentioned that I spent a considerable proportion of my time just talking to staff, helping them refine their roles, along with their managers, to achieve a little more flexibility. My take was that keeping staff happy would, in turn, result in greater productivity. I shared an example of how we stopped selling cars that were over three years old. Instead, we kept them on fleet and allowed staff to run these without charge, thereby limiting or eliminating their reliance on public transport. Another approach was to offer them loans (within the parameters of the HMRC, of course), to help them with things they needed.

The CEO branded me an idiot. His view was clear-cut: who has the time to talk to staff when you are running a business? He then went on to ridicule the car policy, believing that none of his staff would want a car that was over three years old, with high mileage.

Having taken the opportunity to get to know my staff better, I recognised that they were not robots here to serve me. They were in employment to make a life for themselves and add value to the Company, too. When a staff member resigns, it affects so many things: a recruitment fee for their replacement, training costs, impact on other staff, impact on general morale and ineffective time before new hires are proficient.

One day, one of my team informed me that he was interviewing a person from the same organisation the CEO I referred to above was from. I was rather curious, so I asked if I could sit in.

I found out that the Company offered great facilities, more than we could offer. Yet, somehow, the candidate was not happy there.

People were far too busy to take lunch breaks or lounge in a comfy chair and, if you did, they piled on more work as you clearly had free time … you get the message.

Creating a great culture starts with one thing, a Leader who really believes and understands the value of people, not worker drones, but people, for all their faults, ambitions and greed. We are all human.

Fail to recognise people's natural needs and desires, they will seek recognition elsewhere. And they do.

GET OUTRAGEOUS AND KEEP IT REAL

There is nothing wrong with change, although change for the sake of it can be damaging.

I have had to remind myself of this many times over the years. On many occasions, I was brought in to change something in large Companies. Yet, when I arrived, I realised that the changes needed were quite straight forward, and were completed within a few months.

Being a Leader who likes change, the tendency is to then seek out more to change or fix.

In the event the Company or division you are running is operating fine, it is sometimes necessary to just let it run without further changes.

There was one time a multi-billion pound Global Company approached me for support. They needed me to fix some issues in one of their divisions. I was sold on a story of woe, a troubled past involving people, clients, supply and risk. I thought this interesting and was glad to help.

When I arrived, there was only one problem.

It all boiled down to two senior staff, who were dragging everyone down with their poisonous, negative, doomy outlook. Sort of like a weather forecaster who frequently complains about the little warmth or rain in England, despite that being rather normal. You know the sort of person I mean. They needed to go, and fast.

So, cutting through the crap and exiting these people is what I did, promoting others up within the organisation. I then faced the wrath of the Board, as I had dared to dismiss two people, something that was unheard of in this organisation.

Perhaps there was a bigger problem – the President himself! (No, I am not referring to the US elections).

Seriously though, within three months of implementing this change, some six months after I joined, we were making strong progress, as strong as other divisions in the group. Things were now working, and I needed to keep it this way.

Although, with little chance of displacing the UK President, my options were limited.

In fact, my options were limited to stay and watch something simple work well, or leave. I chose to leave as I did not feel my problem-solving skills were required, which is not the choice some would have made.

Setting realistic and truthful goals is fundamental to attracting and retaining the right skill set for the organisation. If not done properly, mismatches become obvious and are noted.

Setting unrealistic goals may be the reason staff choose to leave. For them, the reason for being there soon rests on shaky foundations, on false hope. Like a dream that one knows will never materialise.

So, is this a bad thing, then? Having a dream is never a bad thing. Having an outrageous ambition, something that must be achieved, though, is quite a stretch.

To make all or part of this ambition materialise, one should make their goals absolutely clear so that colleagues can share the dream. But there needs to be a reality attached.

For example:

If your goal was the same as your outrageous ambition, it's likely for problems to arise. If one's outrageous ambition was to be the best supplier of a product in every country in the world, as well as to offer part ownership to staff, something which is beyond the remit of any powers, then it's unlikely to materialise. As such, year after year, one would fail.

This would have less of an impact if it were an outrageous ambition. But, as a corporate goal, the consequential continued failure would not be healthy for staff, or yourself as the Leader, of course.

I am not suggesting that you make your goals easier to achieve. All I suggest is that the goals are ones that staff can relate to, something that can be achieved with considerable effort.

So how do you make goals realistic?

I hear some colleagues describe this as climbing a mountain, or eating an elephant.

Neither of these seem like pleasant pastimes to me, I can assure you. Although, breaking down a mammoth (no pun intended) task into bite-sized chunks is easier to focus on, more relative to people, and likely to be achievable with the right inputs from those who play a considerable role in getting there – your team.

As I said, having a dream or an outrageous ambition is a good thing, but one needs to keep these separate to allow ordinary, more everyday goals to be achieved. Dreams are just that.

Let's return to the subject of staff engagement. Again, setting goals is a positive step.

Similarly, as mentioned, having dreams can be healthy too. A milkman's dream of starting up their own multi-national Software business, being CEO and 100% Shareholder, may just be a dream. Instead of reminding the milkman of his underachievement on a monthly basis, setting realistic goals, things the milkman can tangibly work towards, small progressive steps towards bigger achievements, is often a better strategy.

Achieving goals that are a stretch but within reach, is uplifting for many. Choosing the right goal for people with different skills is fundamental to this, though.

Ask yourself whether this goal is something they can influence themselves? If not, there is a strong chance they may give up before starting, which would be a waste of time.

I once spoke to a Sales Director in my outsourcing days. He implemented the 1-2-1 monthly meeting process and told me that the process of monthly goal setting, and monthly meetings, were a waste of time (well, they probably were the way he was doing them).

I looked at the goals he'd set for his team members before focusing on one (they were all similar). It read, 'Hit your target.'

Now, you can imagine that most people would be frustrated with this statement. For instance, say the sales person hit their target three times in a year, but came close on nine other occasions. Overall, in the scheme of things, this is still considered good performance, but the sales person left after a year, despite earning good commission and performing better than some of his or her peers.

Failure is the underlying theme they hear

from their managers. Well, of course, what else would you expect?

If the goals were more tangible (and believe me they were changed in this instance) and broken down by what the individual needed to do or achieve in order to progress that month, they would be more realistic. An example would be to have the following goals: call customer A, make a revised offer of X, make Y number of follow up calls regarding the latest campaign, demonstrate to Prospect 3 the service on offer by introducing to Client 4.

These things are tangible, and quantifiable. Even if a target is not met, you can maintain the person's motivation, analyse which parts failed and offer help or guidance via their direct managers. Through this process, an understanding of one's failure to achieve their goals would become more apparent.

This is what I meant when I said it would be better to break a problem down into its component parts.

I once had an experienced MD working in my team. His failure, in my opinion, was his lack of productivity (which we fixed, of course). He blamed this on a multitude of persistent issues (hey, welcome to management).

It is quite common for the human brain to want to do the small tasks, while pushing the bigger, more important issues to another time (you know, when you have a spare week or so!).

Subsequently, the more important tasks are likely to fall through the cracks and are not addressed, persistently left on the to-do list, and certainly never leaves the brain as a completed project.

We should not be too harsh here, as this truly is quite common in many aspects of life.

So, we decided to embark upon an exercise together, which did help resolve this. We came up with a simple, productive process that, when followed, worked a treat.

The process involved recognition of the fact that the Director worked quite well on the small stuff (which we all typically do). Acknowledging this, we broke the bigger problem down into little pieces.

He said, 'Okay, you are now branding me as a simpleton, and stating the obvious.' I reassured him that these challenges were common among Leaders and managers. These roles are inherently subjected to constant bombardment of challenges, leaving Leaders and managers reacting to each thing as it happens. In the process, the big problems or 'next developments' get shelved for another day when there is more time, which, invariably, they never really have.

So, we broke the unachieved challenge into its component parts, some of which needed other people's input and some relied on the completion of other tasks. We found that some tasks could be done that same month, right away even, which, overall, moved us one step closer to addressing the bigger problem. Going forward, each month we did the same thing.

Although, the MD did say to me, 'This is not Leadership. You are turning me into a glorified bloody project manager.'

Well, the process we followed did reflect similar project management concepts. But, what was the alternative? Continued Leadership of his Division with failure, or try something new? One would receive my support; the other would cost him his job.

In the end, he followed my path, but reluctantly at first. Then sporadically at times. Throughout this, I kept him on track. Perhaps I was the master Project Manager. At the end of the day, who gives a shit what we are called? It is the impact we make that counts.

Four months later, we were much closer to fixing the major problem in its entirety. So much so, in fact, that we were now evolving the project into making it better, adding new things just for fun and improvement, because we could.

The MD came to recognise that this process had helped him. Sadly, though, he never seemed to be able follow this process without a constant kick up the arse, or a reminder of why we were doing this.

But this is management, the part of the role that needs us to measure, monitor and focus people so they can perform in their roles effectively.

When people ask me if I am a manager or Leader, I always state that I must be both. The point they're trying to make is: can you step up to Lead when required, or are you just a manager?

Keeping things on track is management (which itself requires great skills), leading people towards change without unilateral decision-making to achieve betterment is Leadership.

LET'S GET ALL STRATEGIC

So, let's say that you have built a team. They are good, the best you can find or afford. Then you task them with producing something for distribution to the rest of the Company. For instance, a strategy document. 'Lovely,' I hear you say.

But not necessarily so.

Let's say a strategy document is issued by the marketing department. It invariably comprises the views and beliefs of that function, which is great in itself, but how, in reality, does this link in with other teams or functions?

In truth, often it does not. Inevitably, over the course of time, we experience conflict, politics and poor results. Why? Well, creating a strategy document requires interweaving with the wider

Company strategies. This helps to bring in the marketing strategy, and it is understood by all other teams. I am not picking on marketing, I'm just using it as an example. This would be the case for any department tasked with the creation of a strategy document.

There is no point in the marketing team proposing a path that the sales department cannot wholeheartedly support, or one the delivery teams cannot bring to life easily, or within the time frames specified.

Of course, each department needs to know what to work on, and what to do in order to follow the right path. The key phrase is 'the right path'. It should resonate with the path other teams follow, otherwise such diverse movements create unnecessary conflict and inertia.

Additionally, the word 'strategy' is often misused; it should be a way of defining what steps to take in order to move from point A to point B.

Even if just one team moves along a different path to other teams, you will face difficulties when attempting to merge these to one common set of strategies.

A CEO once turned up to one of our m board meetings, full of drive and energy so than usual), despite a trail of months where we failed to achieve the goals that had been set.

He said, 'Today, we start our new strategy to achieve our growth … to open 10 more offices and a new division within six months.' This immediately raised questions: was this a fix for the current ineffective strategy? Was it a replacement of our current goal? Or, given our poor performance to date, how would we fund this?

The key element at the time was the question 'how?'. How do we achieve this?

This is the biggest single failure commonly seen in CEO's and their teams. The error lies in not breaking down the directive through presenting the specifics that need to be delivered by individuals or teams. This alone would transform a dictation into action, with measurable outcomes.

The next point is 'why?'. Why do we need to do this? Why are we thinking of this? I will cover this in other sections.

Let's put the question of what needs to be done into more context.

If you set a goal for an individual to open one more office, there is a strong chance they will not share the same vision. They might interpret the message differently, and possibly lack the knowledge or direction on how to generate the required outcome.

This is where a detailed strategy would be beneficial, through a clear set of actions required to support the move from A to B. In this example, the strategy should consist of a number of projects and tasks that people can tangibly touch and relate to themselves, and, in doing so, breaking down the journey into smaller, more defined steps that can be measured.

Importantly though, it must be measurable for the person performing the task, otherwise, how do they know they are doing a great job? That they are on the right path?

Similarly, the CEO will need to ensure that all teams are mindful of their contribution potential and limits, as well as their responsibilities.

I often watch police dramas on TV, where the Chief Inspector/FBI Director, or whoever is leading the 'investigation', says to their team, 'We must find this criminal. I want to know where the person has lived for the past 12 years, their known associates. Put a tap on his cards and phones, and monitor airports, roads and any CCTV' ... or other specific criteria.

This is a great example of good, clear instructions. It is certainly more defined than just saying 'catch this nutter quickly'.

At this point in the show, they usually switch to another scene as the Leader darts off to some exotic place. Who is doing what? Who is ensuring that they are not all doing the same thing, bumping into each other and duplicating efforts? Is it that the first person who gets this info is the smug one, and all others are disappointed? Hopefully not, but this scenario is the reality in the business world if people are unclear of their tasks and objectives.

What do I need to do to help us achieve the goal as a team? What specifically do I need to do in relation to others?

Every business, however complex, feel they are unique. And most CEO's believe that their business is unique. Irrelevant to uniqueness, they need people to be doing the right tasks to ensure things don't go horribly wrong.

It is true that businesses are unique in some way, but fundamental functions are generally similar. Holding all this together is their people.

The Leader is responsible for ensuring functional teams work together in a way that supports one another, and to fundamentally unite the team under one set of goals. In doing so, each team is better aligned. Not doing this could result in goals taking longer to achieve or, at worse, complete failure and misalignment.

Setting the strategy to achieve the goals should be done at team level so that each team knows how the other is progressing. It is the responsibility of each Leadership Team member to be closely involved in understanding what other teams are doing and why in order to align the rate of progress, and to challenge each other in making sure they are united in their acceptance of the strategies themselves.

For example, in my outsourcing days, we had thousands of people working in manufacturing. In particular, the automotive manufacturing industry.

I recall marvelling at how well one of the manufacturing facilities was run. Every supply component was delivered on time, and each division worked at the same pace to deliver the final product, a shiny new car.

It really was a fantastic experience to watch and learn from. Yet, occasionally it went wrong. One tiny failure on just one step in the process impacted on the whole production line, resulting in lost time; and lost time meant loss of production within a set timeframe.

This example greatly illustrates what happens when people work together at the same pace for the same goal.

If, in the same facility, marketing and sales did not keep pace with production, production would cease at some point. Conversely, if parts could not be secured in time for production, there would be a reduction in sales.

However, when every step ran smoothly, end to end, productivity was fantastic. Something I believe can be used to demonstrate that teams that work well together can achieve excellent results.

Okay, when it comes to uniting a board on a strategic list of actions, the end product may not be as visible as the production of a car, but the same alignment issues exist. Only, one may not see it until much later.

THE 6 P'S OF BUSINESS

The title of this section might get you thinking of famous book references to clever marketing concepts, six things one must do in order to get their business working well. Oops, this might not be what you you'll be getting, sadly.

In this part of the book, I refer to planning as common sense. Yet, every one of us, at some point in our lives, have failed to get this right.

In my leasing days, I worked for a large Company that was, at the time, one of the largest Companies in the world. It was a hugely successful, multi-faceted business, revered by its peers and competitors globally.

This was a heavily process driven business, and it worked well. Ultimately, it was a very profitable business to be part of.

I had risen to the dizzy heights of running National Accounts. Wow! what a position. I had jumped ahead of those much more senior than me in terms of experience to get this role. I must have been great, right? Well, you will soon note that this was not always so.

The phrase 'National Accounts' in this context referred to major clients, some international. Subsequently, the position allowed for travel in and out of the UK. I had soon become a seasoned traveller (to some; a travel Muppet to others). I regularly visited an enviable client list, meeting senior officials in transport, shipping, retail and manufacturing. With every passing month, I broadened my knowledge of the industry and loved every moment of it.

Today, travel across borders is easier. Although, with Brexit on the horizon, this may change. In my early days, certain places were difficult to travel to and from unless you knew what you were doing.

Cue my next travel arrangements.

I had been travelling regularly and was always well prepared for every business meeting I was to attend. My research was always exemplary, I looked ready, and I was well rehearsed and ready for anything. My cool charm at such a young age was a rare addition. I was so well prepared, even the most challenging of meetings was taken in my stride. It was no wonder I had been promoted so quickly.

Then came the call from our manager in Northern Ireland. Our Global account with a well-known European Shipping business was at risk due to contractual concerns with the trading division outside of Belfast. If this was lost, the impact would be devastating as they were a voice listened to by others in the Group. My secretary (yes, we all had them in those days) was off sick that week. Although my boss had brought in a temporary cover to help, we were not in possession of laptops or smart phones. Email and internet were not used as extensively prior to the 1990s.

However, I politely asked my temporary secretary to book me on a flight to Belfast, where I would be meeting my team and the client's representatives, all four of them in total.

Being more in tune with travel than I was, at least when it came to dealing with travel agents and flight co-ordination, she had asked me where in Belfast I need to be.

It was a strange question, I thought. I was looking to take the first flight out of Luton and return on the last flight. Just a day trip I told her, no hotel required. All I need was for her to get me on the first flight! Which she gladly did.

And so, two days later, I was fully prepared. I had the answers to the client's concerns, and was looking forward to resolving the conflict that had arisen. It clearly required my personal attention, my calming suaveness and charming relaxed smile; that would make all better again. All I needed was 30 minutes with them. Not just to alleviate their concerns, but to ensure my calming influence could impact them in the way that was required. Only our man from London could do this (me), as our local team just did not have the presence and perception of seniority.

It was a meeting I had replayed in my mind several times, while rehearsing and polishing it as usual. I was unstoppable.

At the airport, all was on time and running well. I was due to arrive at the time specified, and my team were due to meet me in Belfast.

The plan was to meet briefly before the client's representatives joined us at the airport, Belfast International.

And so, I was asked for my passport … quite a standard procedure. But, oh shit, passport, no way could I have forgotten this! I had travelled a hundred times by plane, and I had left it behind. How the hell would I explain this? Flight cancelled? No, they could check that. Feeling unwell? A bit lame as I never took time off. I was a workaholic for goodness sake.

I pleaded with the representative to let me on the plane. I was asked to present another photo ID. My passport was the only photo ID I had, so I thought. I checked through my wallet, looking for some magic document, looking for something, anything … and then I saw it.

I offered the representative my Colchester Zoo Annual Gold Card, with an embedded, badly pixelated picture offering me discounted cuddly toys and free entry for a 12-month period. The Gold Card was checked and I was allowed to board (this was pre 9/11 of course). No-one could have been more smug. I wanted to shout about it. Yet my pride, due to my failed preparation, was holding me back. I could not help smiling to myself, though. I like to win.

This was not my first flight to Belfast International. I always took an active interest in the ground from the cabin window seat that I always insisted on.

Circling to land, I did not recognise the view. Perhaps we were on a different flight path, I thought. Eventually, we landed with the usual 'Thank you for travelling with us today, the local time is 1002 a.m. Welcome to Belfast City Airport' (are you paying attention), Belfast CITY Airport. 'Excuse me, miss,' I said, 'did you just say City airport? By that I assume it is Belfast City (it is a city) International Airport?' 'No, sir, it's Belfast City Airport.' ... Oh my god!

In all the panic over my misplaced (okay, forgotten) passport, and my continued smugness at the departure lounge, I had failed to realise I was travelling to the wrong bloody airport. Okay, let's keep calm. I have got this. Belfast International is just around the corner, it will be fine.

I made a brief call to my Irish colleague and explained the error (that the temp had booked the wrong flight!). Then I approached a waiting taxi and asked the driver how long the journey would take. He stammered severely, to my shock, and eventually confirmed it would take an hour.

One hour? I was going to be late. The client would arrive before me, which would not give me the chance to brief my colleagues. Not to worry, I assured myself, I could still get away with this.

My colleague was in a panic but trying hard not to show it. Over the phone, my colleague warned me not to take a black cab from City Airport, but I was not really listening. Thinking I could expense the travel costs, I didn't think much more about it. The Company would pay for me to proceed to Belfast International Airport, but I had failed to understand why he was concerned about the black cab.

Well, his concern was a valid one. Due to historical trouble in Belfast, recent bomb attacks had been launched using black cabs. Primarily because of their universal acceptance across Northern Ireland. And I was travelling in a black cab registered in Bandit country to an area of Nationalist control, where threats had been made … oh shit.

As positive as ever, I left what looked like gangland warfare territory, with its brightly coloured pavements and walls with well-drawn pictures on the sides of houses of gunmen and anti-British slogans, with my taxi driver, hoping he knew how to get Belfast International.

Any attempts at having a dialogue were hopeless, mainly due to his unfortunate stammer. He struggled to present a response to my polite conversation. Still, I was on my way, and I looked good in a neatly pressed three-piece blue suit.

Ah, here we go, signs for Belfast International Airport. I could see the airport ahead. Well, at least I could get a lift back from my local colleagues later in the day, rather than take another expensive taxi.

The driver painfully told me to wind down both my windows in the back (they were manual back in those days) for a security check. Strange, but I complied with the request.

We drove slowly towards a checkpoint, which at the time was of no significance to me at all. I was more interested in the terminal building and called my colleague on my enormous mobile phone, which took up most of my briefcase. 'I have just arrived.' Calls were really expensive then, so I terminated the call after my brief announcement.

As the car gently pulled to a halt, an armed officer approached and placed one hand on the driver's window frame. His other hand was firmly on his pistol, which was still in the holster (you know what's coming, don't you?).

He asked the driver one simple question: 'Is everything alright in there?' nodding towards the back seat (me, in other words). The next few seconds/minutes are a blur; the start of an absolute bloody nightmare.

The driver could not get his words out and, in a panic, raised his hands before he could string a few words together. The guard, well, doing his job I guess, pulled his gun on me, thinking the driver had panicked because I was a terrorist (the audacity of the man!). Suddenly, amidst a stream of expletives, I was told to get on the floor (of the cab) with my hands where they could see them. I did not move. I was rather confused. Then, without warning another soldier appeared at the other window, with an automatic rifle pointing at my head, shouting at me to get on the floor.

Well, I jumped onto that dusty, dirty old floor and lay there, screaming for them not to shoot. Sort of like a petulant, overtired child begging for a bedtime extension.

By the time I looked up, the taxi had been waved on. It turned out that the driver had finally spoken to them and they had been reassured that all was okay.

I was still lying on the floor. My navy blue polished look was now covered in grey dust. I had tears in my eyes from screaming and the fear of having two guns pointed directly at my face. And in all the commotion, the contents of my briefcase had spilled and lay scattered around me.

'Here comes our head of National Accounts now, chaps.' No doubt that would have been the introductory comment to the client's representatives. 'We will soon have everything fixed.' The door opened and in crawled some street urchin. A vagabond with shaking hands (literally shaking not the greeting method) and unable to speak. This person had zero credibility and mimicked the presence of a beggar in a dirty suit, surrounded by bric-à-brac and waste paper.

We did fix the problem, although not on the day. My poor planning had cost me dearly in terms of reputation, and my ignorance to local culture had brought me close to being shot.

So, the 6 P's of business, in my opinion, are: Piss Poor Planning Prevents Peak Performance!

Think carefully about what you need to do, plan for the worst and hope for the best.

THE BURNING PLATFORM

Earlier, we talked about what motivates people to do things.

So, let's focus specifically on change.

In transforming organisations, one variable always presents itself as a major challenge: the people.

I was talking to an NHS Consultant recently over dinner, one who has departmental responsibilities. He wanted to know how to get people to change the way they did certain things. The Consultant had been tasked with a new directive in his hospital, which was basically part of a larger initiative to cease taking the traditional, historic, tried and tested approach, and trial a different path.

So, how do you get them to do it?

As mentioned in the opening section of this book, everyone wants a simple answer, a magic formula. Something so simple and easy to deploy, it could be done by anyone. Sadly, nothing is that easy, I explained.

We talked about the need to understand people. Clearly, he was at odds with this. He was a fantastic medical practitioner (seriously good), and someone I would hope to be treated by if I ever fell ill. His record had secured the responsibility of leading his own department whilst still being the departmental lead medic. Although, he was not a comfortable Leader (not a criticism, I can assure you. I have the utmost respect for his talents).

Not knowing specific details about the change he was referring to, I took some time to ask him questions. Why would the staff need to do, or not do, things differently? This is where the problem became apparent.

The only reason he could give me was that the CEO had issued an instruction. There was no apparent reasoning outlined in the memo. It just said the change had to be implemented with immediate effect. Sort of like a 'we will be doing it this way' order.

And, as expected, a few weeks later, he was told by his CEO that his department were letting everyone down by sticking to old practices. The CEO ordered the Consultant to get on top of it and report back.

Still, the Consultant was none the wiser as to why the instruction had been issued. There was no doubt that it followed an audit committee decision, or the like and not like unilateral knee jerk from the CEO, but the 'why' was still not clear. My concern was that if it was unclear to him, then it was certainly unclear to his team, too.

'Okay,' he said. 'That's good. I will find out and then tell them,' was his response. This is not the entire journey though. Understanding the reason behind a change is obviously an essential part of this, but what about the need to understand what will happen if one can't or does not initiate the change?

'Ah,' he said, 'so you suggest I threaten them with the sack? This is the NHS, and good people are hard to find. I will not be able to fire them for not following orders, unless lives are endangered by their actions. That's just not practical.'

I was not talking about sacking them for insubordination (in this case, at least). I was referring to offering them an explanation on the implications of not accepting that a change was needed. Companies and trainers who practice 6-Sigma call this the Burning Platform.

I want you to picture a platform (an oil rig maybe) in the sea. The shore is in sight, with just several hundred meters of deep water in between. Waters known to be inhabited by the odd shark or two.

Naturally, those accustomed to living on the platform were in relative comfort and safety. If the CEO turned around one day and told them there were no helicopters and that, if they wanted to leave, they would need to swim to shore, very few would leave. They would rather be unhappy and live with the relative safety of the platform, in preference to the imminent perceived threat.

Instead, if the CEO announced the presence of an uncontrollable fire on the platform, and told everyone they'd die within minutes, the number of people jumping into the unknown would soon grow exponentially. Staying on the platform would no longer be an option. They would take this step despite the unknowns and potential risks that awaited them. In other words, these people would conclude for themselves that the risk of change was less than the risk of staying put.

This is the Burning Platform. Naturally, I would not want anyone to set fire to their desks and say, 'Off you go to your new role as this is clearly illegal and dangerous'. Although, through appropriate staff engagement, this could be addressed better.

So, going back to the Consultant's dilemma. Perhaps there is something that his team would consider riskier than not making the requested changes. What could that be? Given the problems reported about the NHS, would the threat of funding being stopped be a good incentive? Or is the equipment they are using no longer supported, or providing reliable results? Is the process they refuse to move away from preventing them from saving more lives, or helping more patients?

In short, if the decision to change is based on solid reasoning, along with some idea of the benefits and impacts, let's share it. People may not always like it, but they will jump if given a compelling enough reason.

Our role as the Leader is not to issue instructions and then demand it to attract everyone's admiration. It is to take people with you on a journey.

Ideally, if teams are engaged properly, they will already be aware of the reasoning behind a change, what options were considered and, importantly, the impact of not implementing a change.

This approach will generate feedback, which may prove to be more time consuming initially. Just remember that you are not on a mission to gather everyone's signed agreement of the change (although, this could be helpful), as this may never get completed.

A Leader is there to explain the reasoning, to secure the backing of most people. Get the masses with you, and they will help you convince the doubters wherever possible.

If the reason to change is strong enough, they will see common sense.

In my Software days, I took over at a point where we were losing money fast. It was very clear that we would run out of money within a few months if nothing changed.

I highlighted the problem to staff, which was a shock as they had been kept in the dark to this point. I also highlighted a detailed plan we would need to adopt if we wanted to succeed. The plan clearly indicated how individuals could contribute, so any panic could be tempered with a journey to recovery.

After the initial shock, a different team emerged, generally speaking.

They recognised that the Company had not been managed well, and, with new energy and focus, they could help turn around the Company's fortunes by doing their bit.

We experienced a magical time of ideas and thoughts, and had endless helpful suggestions from staff. They even offered to take on more responsibility, with very few asking for anything in return.

We were a team united, with fear at our core.

A fear of failure? Maybe, but definitely a fear of losing their jobs. The potential loss of a culture they had become familiar with, a culture they enjoyed in the main and a culture they wanted to maintain.

So, to avoid having changes being forced on them, they accepted the problems and did the best they could in doing their bit to turn the Company around. In doing so, they accepted change for the right reasons. They had chosen to jump from comfort and follow me to shore through the unknown. I had offered them more security (well, as much as any Leader can, I suppose).

Through this mindset, they became part of the solution. I had promised nothing other than complete honesty, openness and a 'warts and all' update on progress every month, which I continued to provide.

Although we are the Leaders, we are human too. By putting yourself in the shoes of your team and offering them an explanation and openness, as well as sharing your journey and the reasoning, people will follow you with little or no conflict.

FEAR, GREED AND SEX

We all have our own drivers, our own reasons for doing things and, as humans, we are programmed with some basic instincts. Some of us exhibit these more than others.

The levels or extremities of these behaviours may change over time, but we all have them.

For example, I know of sales organisations that focus on greed. There is nothing wrong with aiming high and wanting to do well, earn a good living and reward yourself with luxuries, the spoils of war, like taking a holiday to relax after a stressful six months. Later in life, we may take on more responsibilities, such as becoming a parent, or buying a house or two. Our basic needs then become driven by different demands, fuelled by the need to maintain the lifestyle. Money is the key. Or is it?

I am not saying that freedom to be a capitalist is wrong. Far from it. Money does make the world go around, etc. But staff engagement is not about a one size fits all. People are different.

A friend of mine works within a Pyramid sales structure (where one person sells to three, who in turn sells to five, and they all earn). Although, this concept is no longer referred to as 'Pyramid selling', due to bad publicity. It is now called an inverted triangle model. Apparently renamed to eliminate bad press (are they for real?).

So, this friend of mine is reasonably well off (certainly by comparison to their peers in this structure). They seem to have everything they need in life.

Over the course of a training session, which was aimed at helping them sell more, jump higher and run faster (the usual stuff), they were asked to complete a story board. They were told to use magazine cut outs to illustrate their dreams, desires and where they wanted to be in life. I recall doing this myself when I was selling financial services, life insurance, pensions, etc. … early on in my career.

The trainer expects to see cut outs of glamorous people, beautiful and well dressed, a yacht maybe, kids in a private school (or independent school as we call it nowadays). There will most certainly be an expensive car, maybe a supercar, a red Ferrari – oh nice.

Cut outs of houses will not necessarily include a mansion, but something one can see themselves owning, something similar to what your new acquaintance has (I would say best friend, but you hate them so much for having it). Likewise, there are usually cut outs of idyllic beaches with no one on them, just two sun beds and a bottle of champagne next to two full flutes, gently effervescing, awaiting your undivided attention.

Yes, that's what I want. These are my dreams. Well, take a ticket my friend. It's a stereotypical human greed story, and sales companies know it.

But how do you get there? You guessed it! Sell, sell, sell; sell more than you believe possible and we will show you how. It takes self-belief and aggression. Do not take no for an answer, sell to your friends, sell your bloody grandma if you have to. I saw all this 25 years ago, but nothing has changed. Why? Well, because human drivers have not changed, and why would they? It takes longer than this for real evolution.

Well, my friend has what they need, does not want a Ferrari (they could sell one to me for a £1 if they wanted to). Instead, they buy a new car every 2-3 years, take lovely holidays twice a year and live debt free, with kids at independent schools.

All they want is to carry on with enough to manage financially. Their need is no greater than the desire to be part of something or belong to a group. They want to share knowledge, be liked and have some independence from their spouse and children, including some social interactions.

They were far from motivated following the training course. It had quite the opposite effect. My happy and content friend came out thinking they were a failure. They were not doing enough, not achieving much, and were uninspiring to their 'triangular' colleagues. They also felt as though they had little to contribute in conversations, social events or similar training courses.

This was a person who had a track record of good sales. Through selling, they had built an indirect network of people and, in my opinion, was previously happy in their work.

When I worked in telecommunications, I remember noting that the greed culture was quite strong.

With 40 competitors all selling into London's square mile, in the same small geographical space, it was quite competitive. Cut throat competition that brought out the best and the worst in people.

I was part of a team of 10 sales people. Again, we were all driven by big rewards and the promise of driving that red Ferrari for the next month. Wow. To the sales person of the month, that would seem like a great symbol of recognition.

The Leader was an aggressive chap who had no time for losers. He was the Alpha, the king pin, the man who knew no failure, or so he thought.

I recall a particularly tense moment when he walked into the office one day and began ranting at the Sales Director (someone we actually respected for his sales ability). An argument ensued. The Leader was clearly unhappy.

We were all on the phones, desperately trying to hit our appointment targets. Some were standing on chairs, to indicate they were behind in hitting their targets. Others were trying desperately to get their four appointments per day for the next four days. If you failed to achieve your target appointment level by the end of the day, the Company took one hundred pounds as a salary deduction (only in the 80s!). When my disastrous call ended, another disaster struck. The MD started a fight with the Sales Director, an actual fist fight, right there in front of us. These were no shrinking violets. They were capable of taking care of themselves (that was obvious from the way they were fighting). Chairs were broken, shirts were ripped and blood-stained but, although the tables in front of us moved, we kept calling. We dialled those bloody phones like our lives depended on it. Even long after the fight was broken up by the FD, who didn't seem to mind the odd judicial punch of authority, we continued our calls, not because we wanted the commission, but because we did not want to get beaten up.

One of my colleagues (ex-navy) did intervene. He tried to calm the fight, and ended up with a broken nose and a dry-cleaning challenge for the local Vietnamese family around the corner.

I was absolutely terrified, terrified of being punched, losing my job and being sacked. It was just pure terror that filled my mind.

This was, after all, an environment where the MD would meet the sales team at 06:30 down at the gym every week. To prove his Alpha status, he would challenge each team member to a fitness competition. In fairness, this guy was like Arnold Schwarzenegger running a double marathon. He was a robotic maniac, and those he beat (all of us really) had to pay him a £100 fine. Naturally, such a thing would be outlawed today, thankfully. But this was the culture at the time. I lived in fear.

I dialled those numbers and sold my shaking little heart out as the MD, with his blood-stained face and shirt, walked around the sales floor. My concentration was on the call, not him. Although, I could not trust him. So, I kept half an eye on him, given that I was worried I'd be his next victim: the nervous, failing sales person, short and weak by comparison, an easy target.

Success followed. I achieved more appointments that week than in the two previous weeks combined. With a few hours to go, I was stacking these appointments up for the coming weeks too. I was on fire. I did not care one hoot about the money from potential sales; I was just focused on surviving the day and escaping unharmed, which, thankfully, I did.

The success that followed reminded me that my driver was not greed but fear. Fear of losing my job, among other things.

This is a common driver, and whilst I do not advocate this at all, we must recognise that fear does drive and deliver outcomes.

If we can find a way of uniting people towards overcoming a common fear, this can be good, providing you get the people behind the journey.

I since realised that this was a great way of engaging staff. Although, the fear needs to be real and relevant, something that can be recognised, shared and addressed.

Something like turning a Company around. Clearly there is a fundamental problem, or why the hell would I be there?

Typically, if a Company, a division or brand is performing badly, there will be repercussions if the performance is not corrected or addressed.

It is important to be open with your staff, highlight where the problems are and why these need to be addressed. By doing this, you unite them with one common goal or outcome. Fear of failure is no bad thing if you can use it to your advantage.

Often, Leaders prefer not to say anything, treat staff like children and reassure them that everything will be alright – even when it is not. Staff are not children, they are strong, independent people making a life for themselves. They will respect being treated with honesty, integrity and fairness. Trusting them openly with issues will achieve better results than keeping them in the dark.

What about the third point, motivation by sex? Well, what this means, I will leave to your imagination. I think this has a different place in life in general, watch out for my next book …

… only joking of course.

BABY STEPS –
LONG JOURNEY

As a Leader, defining what needs to be done is relatively easy. After all, Management Consultants have been thriving on this for decades. I borrow a saying from another Leader, who described Management Consultants as people who ask to borrow your watch so they can tell you the time when you ask. A little harsh on this community (particularly having done this myself), although, you get my point: the answers are there all along.

So, stating that we need to improve sales or increase profits is kind of obvious to most. But this is where genius becomes flawed.

Telling staff that we need to achieve something does not generate sustainable results. For instance, saying that our goal is to be the largest supplier of X to the Y market. As a staff member, I would respond by saying 'that sounds dandy, and I look forward to getting there. But, for now, I will carry on doing what I do as this probably does not affect me'. So, there are clearly a few things missing here.

1. The staff need to be engaged
2. The staff must know how their contribution helps
3. The staff need specific instruction on what they need to do differently and, more importantly, why

When creating a strategy, staff need to be part of it. They must understand what they need to do in order to get from A to B. Otherwise, all you have is a fancy plan that everyone thinks is for someone else, not for them.

This results in poor adherence, with no one following the journey. This is sure to result in ultimate failure as everyone will be doing their own thing, which itself is hard to manage.

Naturally, a person who answers the phone as a trainee administrator may not be able to relate to improving the Company's profits. So, let's look at this.

The person answering calls is the first contact some people will have with your organisation. It is not a dead-end job, or, shall I say, it does not need to be one.

Passing messages for Bob to call Fred may not, in isolation, require much thought. But, if we then ask ourselves where this could go wrong, we might look at this differently. Perhaps even go as far at looking at how we can improve the process a little.

If the person is treated like a messenger boy, that's all they will do. If the person is told that their job is to get as much detail as possible from the caller, to ensure the right person calls them back and, importantly, this person is empowered to flag it to a Director, things will run more smoothly. If the same client calls again, having not received a call back, then, suddenly, the receptionist has a responsibility to escalate.

Picture a scene where the Operations Manager updates the receptionist as to how the returned call went. The receptionist is now aware that he has called the client and answered their query.

I would always expect to be notified by the receptionist when external calls were not returned. Especially if there were complaints about this, with people just not taking the time to return calls.

In my software days, a senior Project Manager (senior in experience and status) received a series of calls from a new client, who, each time, requested an urgent call back. The receptionist brought this to me as a complaint after the third call went unanswered.

After talking to the Project Manager, it turned out that he was waiting for some information before returning the call. However, from the client's perspective, though, he was being ignored. For the receptionist, if they took their job seriously, it would seem as though messages were not getting through, ultimately reflecting badly on them, and it did. The client was within their remit to ask whether their messages were being passed on, therefore doubting the efficacy of the receptionist, and indeed the Company. This situation would then escalate to: I will flag this to the MD as this is unacceptable. How do you think the receptionist feels now?

Empowered, my friend, that's what. They can relax in the knowledge that they have achieved great customer service, and someone else has failed. If they know what they can achieve or contribute, then they will invariably try and do this.

I am not picking on the receptionist, this is just an illustration of a real scenario.

I remember asking the receptionist to get more involved in the call, and not just pass on messages. So, the next time the Project Manager received a call, the reception passed on the following message: return call before 3 p.m. because of X. Other examples include the case of the sales call that she had filtered and rejected (with a note to the relevant person: passing this on in case you want to pursue further), or a call with a sales enquiry, where the receptionist obtained sufficient detail to ensure an effective and thoughtful call back from the sales team, based on facts they had extracted. The front line role the receptionist plays has gone from passing on telephone messages to empowering and helping us sell. This also contributes to creating a better impression of the Company, as they have the power to insist the non-call back protocol includes escalation to a Director if deemed necessary.

Conversely, I once needed to dismiss a Director for not doing their job. This was based on feedback from an administrator who had highlighted that this person had failed to do what was needed on several occasions, over a period of time. When questioned, he told me that he was the Director and she was an administrator. Authority is not something to be abused, nor does it make a person exempt from doing what is right. Doing the right thing is not based on a title.

Business is like a Swiss watch (not one of those digital display things that work from your smart phone), and people need to understand that each moving part is essential or, if there is no part to play, it is redundant.

In such a small space, there is no room for housing a spare part (sound familiar yet). It also needs to be understood that, unless one part moves, others will cease to move, rendering the device rather useless.

This example (as cheesy as it is), is a good way of highlighting that every piece, however small they may seem at first, plays a vital role. Making sure they work together is the role of the Leader. This is done by ensuring the pace works for all, that everyone is working towards a common goal, and that, if one stops, they all become ineffective.

The team fails when the smaller cog looks at the glossy watch face and thinks to itself, why bother moving, no one sees me, I am invisible, small and have no glamour.

This is particularly important for those who are in the public domain, the Leader included. It's important to recognise that, without each moving part, including the ones behind the scenes, they themselves are ineffective.

This is the reason the Leader must take time to engage all staff in some way (either directly or indirectly via a defined structure), as they are not the most important part, just the most visible.

This is the only way the pace of the business can improve. In other words, you are only as fast as your slowest moving part.

In many Companies, I have adopted Lean and 6-Sigma processes, eliminating waste. There is an interesting exercise that the Operations

Director led with all teams, which involved building a small structure using clip-together parts. Throughout the years, I have adopted this and the exercise has changed somewhat, although the inference remains.

The objective is to task the team with instructions to build something. Working in teams they have to produce a finished product and deliver it to the client (well, to the person in the next room or table).

It was obvious that, by making a production line of people doing each thing well (focus on one thing), the production line sped up (just like in car manufacturing). Equally, it failed miserably when one person failed at their specific task. The knock-on effect was devastating.

Regardless of whether one is making a product or delivering a service, ensuring teams work together can be difficult. As a Leader, seeing and measuring performance improvements over the course of time can be very rewarding.

This exercise has served as a reminder to me that, often, when a person is failing, despite trying hard, changing their role to play to their strengths or interests can have super-positive outcomes.

SUPERMAN LIVES: THE ROLE OF THE CEO

If you read the job description of an MD, or CEO, it should come across as being quite short. In a nutshell, the job requirements are to devise and deliver the strategic objectives agreed with the board/shareholders. Delivery of the objectives should be through empowering people, building and leading teams, corporate governance and total responsibility for everything. Phew, I have finished. But, I have read some job descriptions that go on and on and on, with an endless list of tasks that would, quite frankly, put most people off.

Well, I guess it is good to be clear of what is expected, I hear you say. Yes, of course it is, and ambiguity is never a good thing when it comes to setting objectives with people.

The interviews I have attended, however, have very often highlighted that the panel, the board of Shareholders, expect the applicant to be able to perform each task themselves (to be good at every function). What? How crazy! That's why we have teams, is it not?

Having said that, I do know MD's of mid-sized companies who try hard to be all of this and more, working excessive hours to get it all done.

The comparison is the street performer, who, in the days of old, would be rigged up to a set of strings and instruments, drum, horn, symbols, etc. They would be seen as trying to master the tunes whilst clanking and hooting as he (or she) walked along the street singing. Effectively, portraying a self-sufficient, one man orchestra – exhausting stuff, really, and hugely limited. Especially as there are other talented musicians standing around taking it all in, enjoying the ride. Free entertainment for them, and they'd be getting paid to whine and bitch about the performance behind the other's back.

On the flip side is a person who truly relies on the other band members. Someone who knows their limitations and cannot or does not want to perform on their behalf. Instead, they master and refine the output with intelligence, working a little smarter, meaning they are not completely indispensable.

Ah, well. Maybe this is it. The reason they are performing alone is down to their own insecurity. After all, someone that great cannot be replaced, sacked, or, at the very least, they'd be hugely missed. What would happen to the rest of us if they left?

This is a totally recognisable human trait. It is linked to personal survival. Perhaps even our purpose in life?

Being a Leader, however, is a role that focuses on getting the best out of others to achieve the goals, through utilising the talents of those around us. This is a Leader's talent, something not often understood by hiring boards or agencies, sadly.

Being able to recognise a person's talent before they do is not a talent possessed by all. It plays its own essential role in any Company, along with many other parts.

Many years ago, I was talking to a board in my Fleet Management days. The board meeting was going well, we had achieved so much following the last meeting, now that my team had been in place for a few months. I was delighted with the progress, recognising the achievements of each of my seven reports (you know where this is going now).

Then, one Shareholder asked the question: I can see that this has been a good month for the Company. What have you delivered personally? So, I had taken a failing part of the Company, their Company, restructured it, put the right skills in place and was shaping each team in an effective and productive way ... so, what had I done? He looked like a character from a Charles Dickens' story, sitting there in his sea of discontent, looking judgementally at me, having neither the skill or the character to do what I had done to this point. So, what had I done? I could have forgiven his ignorance at this point, but the next step really sealed my disrespect for him. He then proceeded to list several tasks that he insisted I complete myself, as they could not 'carry anyone'. These tasks were at complete odds to the tasks and objectives for my team. Therefore, at odds with my own tasks as, naturally, I was involved and was part of the work they had done.

I refused on this basis, and on the incredulous response from this geriatric ward of the psychiatric hospital, who seemed to be on a mission to self-destruct, surely?

In real terms, they did not recognise what a Leader was charged to do. I had some empathy with them (okay, not much), as they were limited in their knowledge. They were expecting Superman and his Super team, not a super-managed team.

Wearing my underpants in this way is not something that suits me at all. I continued to be the Director I know, rather than complete the tasks they'd dictated for the sake of trying to manage me. Well, I have yet to meet a decent Leader that is easily managed. So, good luck with that one!

In fact, when a Leader is too engrossed in the detail, it is impossible to remain truly objective. We must create space for ourselves, allow for thinking time, learning time, and give ourselves the opportunity to work on the business, not just within it.

A friend, who was also a Leader, once shared his views of his first MD role. You start off busy, hectic, with no room to think. Then suddenly, your team kick in. They start taking great charge of all the things you once did, and you find yourself with little to do. At this point, the Leader will move on to new, complementary things, and focus on new channels for growing the Company beyond its current positioning. But this only happens if you create the space to do this.

As a massive movie fan, I have watched many films that depict the Leader/king figure on the battlefield, charging his people with emotion (staff engagement), with reason to move (the Burning Platform) and with passion for the task ahead (creating the journey together). They are fired up to move (motivated), to maim and kill at the word of this person (belief in the why). They are ready. The King sets off at speed, hoping his people follow, and they do. Not only do they follow, but they ALWAYS overtake him, ensuring they are first on the scene and taking charge of what needs to be done.

Now, in the business world, the role of the Leader should follow a similar pattern, but it also requires observation, reflection and the ability to react when things happen. The Leader should be in a position to issue instructions from the rear when necessary, from the observation point. This allows him to lead the next charge for the troops, and the process starts over.

All too often, we read job descriptions about someone who must lead from the front. This must be short-lived if a Company is to grow. If the Leader is always busy fighting, how can they find time to work on the next move, the next challenge, opportunity or direction, or, in the very worst case, the survival strategy to fight the next battle.

DON'T TALK TO ME LIKE THAT, I AM A DIRECTOR

Let us not underestimate the responsibilities that go with the job of a Director. Often, the responsibilities are thankless tasks (even in a profit-making business), as you are in a lonely place. You must be objective, and possess the ability to make decisions that will always have an impact on something or someone. Friendships are a rare treat in the early days of a business turnaround as sentiment can be an obstacle when making and enforcing the decisions that previous management failed to deliver. Why else would they need it turning around, eh?

So, enter the lone wolf. Confident, focused, selfish and determined to get what it wants, regardless of the obstacles in its path. The wolf comes with an insatiable hunger for change, for results and betterment, whilst those around wait in anticipation for it to strike, which it will, for sure. Who will it strike at, though?

The job is not an easy one, but acting on processes or people that are just not working well is necessary. It requires clinical focus and a passionate belief that change is done to preserve and protect the rest. After all, even a Leader needs to sleep at night, so they strike for the greater good, not with selfish motives.

Generally speaking, the first rule is not to strike at the staff, most of who are or were following instructions, perhaps incorrectly or being unaware of the repercussions. Nonetheless, they were following an instruction.

It is, therefore, the Leadership function that the Leader must analyse. What are these instructions? How were they founded? And who issued them?

Most of this will be based on sound principles and beliefs, not with malicious intent to cause problems. So, a delicate approach is required. Yet, a firm path needs to be laid out, or else the existing Directors will not deviate. After all, we do employ Directors to direct. By the very nature of the job, such individuals will not be shrinking violets or corporate sheep.

To be able to challenge current methods and responsibilities, something special is required. It is a skill set that most Companies have, but it is often squashed or contained, left in a corner – the outspoken one!

A board that needs change, cannot do so with a bunch of people sitting comfortably in their own cotton wool cladded bubbles that allow them to use their years of charm, negotiation tactics and presence to preserve themselves. I knew a Director many years ago, who we nicknamed Teflon Ron, as nothing seemed to stick to him.

Yes, he sat in judgement, while all around him, staff created disaster upon disaster, failures and successes. My colleagues revered him. He was 'God 2' to the CEO in our wider structure, but, in reality, he was the real source of corporate power.

'Wow, what a great guy,' they would say, suggesting that he was the all-empowered example of a board Director. I felt as if I was in a field on my own, listening to some minion who was suckling on the teat of Teflon Ron, feeding off whatever corporate crap he gave them.

Why could they not see what I saw? A failing Company under his supposed, ineffective Leadership.

After a while, I knew what it meant to be on the receiving end of his empowerment. I nearly lost my job for being outspoken, almost insolent, in his eyes. Success to him was his selfish need for power, not the sustained progressive performance that kept the wheels turning, and people in jobs.

Despite this, in my opinion, I knew he was just a man doing a job, albeit badly. It was high time that he took responsibility for the poorly performing Company that kept us all awake at night with feelings of worry, insecurity and active searching for new jobs.

That's it then. The role of the Director is to take responsibility, responsibility for the actions of the teams, the results of the Company and for overcoming the challenges that are never ending.

This is not the only example of this. I have seen this happen countless times. It still shocks me, to be honest, when I see that blame is pushed onto staff members before the Director stares at themselves in the mirror.

Back to the point regarding the outspoken one.

Find your outspoken one and promote them. Include them and let them have a voice. Dangerous move? Some Leaders fear this person and will avoid them like they would a plague-ridden Londoner from centuries ago. Maybe they are dangerous, but to who and what? In the absence of someone like this, you are just a Leader surrounded by Teflon Rons at worse, cliques in the board room and, potentially, a load of 'yes' people satisfying the Leader who needs to hear nice things and have people do what they are told, regardless of the outcome.

Change needs challenge and sensible thought provoking dialogues that challenge the Directors.

Don't get me wrong, none of your team thank you for this act of pain and torture (Burning Platform – set them alight and see how they react). Sadly, when change is needed, it is often the Directors who need it the most.

I have typically created opportunities for new Directors to join, some through promotion, making sure that my Leadership Team has a good mix of skills and characters. Not all of them are easy to manage.

I remember being brought into a board meeting many years ago. I was honoured, privileged and had found a sense of immense responsibility. I had been chosen. I had been recognised and selected from among many peers within this £1bn turnover group to join the board meetings quarterly (they met monthly).

The President and I talked. I had started to express what an honour it was for me, but he cut me short.

He referred to me as the cuckoo in his nest. How endearing, I thought. He thinks I'm a cute little bird character he can feed, nurture and grow ... hang on a minute. What the hell does he mean?

Well, to be frank, he needed my outspokenness to influence and challenge his board (okay, I was also expected to report to them as well). My results were good, I was on a roll, dynamic in nature and full of opinions (not all of them respectful). They were static, slow to react, old school and failing, quite frankly.

To my surprise, the Directors seemed both resentful and fearful of my involvement. The President was listening to me (well, at least, hearing what I had to say). I was dangerous to some, a loose cannon, someone who would and could turf them out of their cosy nest through my challenging style and opinionated questioning – ah, now I see why he called me a cuckoo.

I served no functional responsibility on this board, other than to help steer change, something I was thankful for, even if I did not understand it at the time. I was facing a Leader who understood this point well enough to endure my opinions and, in the process, invited in challenge. He was a good Leader.

So, in turn, I have adopted this approach, and very successfully. However, when a non-Director is appointed to the board (as a Director Designate or internal promotion), and challenges a Director on how the issues are being dealt with, they are met with terse responses or body language indicating 'who are you to talk to me like that – I am the Director'. This still astounds me.

I have always taken a different view. Yes, let's revert back to staff engagement again.

A Director or Leader is in place to make things work well. Directors are often people with an enormous level of responsibility. Yet, they are still just people, not Gods or miracle workers. They are as imperfect as any other human.

We must recognise that our successes or failures reflect the actions of our staff and the decisions we make and, in doing so, we must be accountable.

Directors are indeed accountable for statutory processes. Being ignorant to this can prove to be very costly and threatening.

I also believe that we are accountable to our teams, the people who help make or break the business. If these people are not fired up, and walking along the same path, our challenges become far too great.

Why, then, do we not take more time to work with them, help them understand our challenges as Directors and show them what we are up against?

Fear of it coming across as weakness? Fear of them finding other uses with this additional information? Fear of them leaving if they knew too much? Yes, these are all genuine fears Directors have.

Picture a scene where the staff are aware of the Company's challenges, its poor performance, its legal battle with a client and its diminishing margins from raw material price increases.

Sadly, some staff find this worrying. However, you will discover a team of people that feel valued, trusted. It is these people who will want to stay on and make a difference, and not just for their own benefit.

I have always been impressed with how engaging staff are in return when such things are shared openly.

Also amazing is the number of people who have approached me to ask what more they can do to help. When you share your challenges in this way, others will see a void to fill, and many will offer to step up.

Often when staff feel that everything is ticking along just fine, they tick along just fine, too.

People are amazing, resilient, resourceful and truly talented.

Our job as their Leader is to discover their potential. This can be done through engaging them and their ideas, listening with a view to change, and making it happen. The Leader can take accountability for leading this and not leave the staff hanging out to dry like a 'Teflon Ron'. Our succession planning originates from seeing the greatness in others and giving them the chance to help and showcase their talents.

Recognising that as a Leader can only be done if you take the time to know the people, and their capabilities, around you. Find ways to engage this, deploy it, and create long-term value through reward and loyalty. Be open. You are just a person among others. You have the power to unite the teams that come together to create something better.

Taking yourself too seriously all the time, perhaps by dishing out your business card, is not inspiring to your teams. Give them a voice, let them criticise. So what if you are the CEO, help them understand what you are up against. They will help if they care, and many of them do.

THE THREE 'MARKETEERS'

I have met many Leaders who claim to be self-proclaimed marketers. How wonderful!

Leadership has its own skill set, as does marketing. Admittedly, a Leader should feel passionate about the marketing function, as well as others.

The **first** of the three 'Marketeers' is the Leader who knows what they want, the one who ends up pushing their own agenda beyond the advice of the expert 'Marketeer'. Earlier, we talked about a Leader migrating towards a specific function in times of stress, and the associated dangers of this.

Marketing can be fun. Creating a new message, a new strapline or even re-branding your image, requires the Leader to be involved and driving this change. The role of the Leader, however, is not to create things themselves, but to drive the change based on the long-term agenda.

Recognising the talents of others can be hard, but for a seasoned Leader, it should come as second nature, and a priority one at that. This requires the ability to recognise the things that someone is not so great at, versus those they are better at.

The **Second** of the bunch is a Leader who recognises the talent of the expert.

I like to believe that someone who specialises in marketing (just an example), will be passionate, knowledgeable and effective in their speciality function. Let's be honest, the NHS runs on the principle of having GPs and specialists. It wouldn't be good for a patient if a career GP decided to specialise one random day because they had some spare time, before returning to their job as a GP the following day.

The same is true with marketing (although, there's no doubt about the health risks, they are just not immediate). A true marketing professional will research what is or is not working in the industry. They will then think differently and act on what is likely to result in a positive outcome, rather than focus on what looks good or let things carry on the way they did in the past.

I have seen the impact of this so many times, and I continue to expect this regularly in the capacity of an adviser.

I once met with a Chairman over dinner at his house. He had been a Marketing Director some 30 years prior. During dinner, he asked questions pertaining to why we had changed our stance from cold calls to nurture campaigns, stressing the point that we were doomed to failure as we had ceased cold calling to promote our services.

He cited how 100 calls a day had resulted in generating three leads in the mid-eighties. Oh, exciting, I thought. Yes, maybe in 1987.

It was now three decades later, and things had moved on. Why, then, was the Chairman stuck in a time zone that was no longer relevant? For the same reason. I also thought I was good at marketing, and had not moved on with my thinking in this area.

If we can recognise that the skills of a Leader must have evolved significantly (or they should have in 30 years), then the marketing function must also have moved on. Consumers and buyers have become more knowledgeable, more refined and less tolerant to techniques used 30 years ago.

I worked in the square mile of the City decades ago, where marketing activity involved walking into buildings, collecting compliment slips and contact details for later use when writing letters and sending faxes before the cold call. I was quite good at this compared to others in my Company, and I achieved great results this way at the time.

I would, however, be a disaster today if I were to use the same techniques. It is the buyer that has moved on. As they have become more sophisticated, and so must we.

I attended a course run on behalf of a large Software Company, aimed at transforming the way software and technology solutions are marketed. It involved NO cold calls or immediate pro-active follow ups for people clicking on the web site.

The techniques included (among many others) putting information out onto the World Wide Web. What? Give buyers free information without meeting them, shaking their hands and looking into the whites of their eyes? Yes, they meant it.

To the shock of many, putting this into practice through providing market details, industry trends, pricing and offers all in exchange for a mere few details, seemed rather strange to the untrained, self-proclaimed 'Marketeer'. As we could see who (or at least which companies) were looking at our web site, surely we should get our sales team to jump on the phone in seconds and pin them down for a sale? Followed by a meeting at least? But no, that was not allowed.

'Nurturing', in this context, involved communicating with the consumer or buyer without demanding anything immediate in return, other than some basic facts. These facts would then be used to inform them about what was on offer specific to their interests or needs, gradually engaging them on an arm's length basis. It started to work. Who knew, eh! Even good sofa sales people do this now.

The outcome of this way of operating over the next year surprised me. It also highlighted that, just like my progressive Leadership skills,

I needed to recognise the progressive nature of the marketing team, the need for new thinking, new input and drive based on next techniques. Someone who was successful 10 years ago, would be of no use to me now in performing techniques of the past.

Similarly, marketing professionals need to keep abreast with changes and not remain on the same page of strategy for life.

On this point, I worked with a PR agency who were commissioned to take our brand to market, raise publicity about us and, ultimately, make the phone ring more often.

They regularly wrote articles on our behalf; they were everything they promised. The articles were well written, full of content and informative, but the effectiveness of these articles were difficult to measure. The phone did not ring in response to these articles. By this, I mean that I do not recall any enquiries being generated from any article. Whether this was because we did not record it, or it just did not happen, is left to your opinion.

However, the Leader needs to take responsibility for this, and that's what I did. I could not really put the blame on the PR Company (although, I may have acted differently if I was put in a corner) as this was my initiative: to bring in the experts. Unfortunately, the PR Company operated in the conventional way, doing things that had generated positive outcomes for many years. They basically followed a process I had been brought up with. Why am I being so generous here by taking responsibility? Pass the buck, surely. It's their fault, not mine, right?

Well, as I had grown up with the belief that PR-based marketing could really up sales for a business, I recognised that all I had to look for in a support service was for them to do what I had asked. So, I purposefully sought a supplier to work the way I was familiar with, rather than being open to new ideas, their ideas.

I had ignored the advice of my Marketing lead, choosing instead to follow my own beliefs. Oh no, I was really becoming conventional, old, going off the boil and losing grip on reality. Sadly, yes.

Recognising my failing, I had to correct it. Yes, the PR agency strategy was failing, but I had enforced this.

I realised that I didn't have the modern marketing expertise I needed. I was a Leader not a marketing expert. After admiring myself and my efforts, I needed to accept that there was a skill gap. There was a generation gap. Yes, I was getting old, but I had moved on, and so had successful marketing.

I received a personal letter from a young man seeking a job. He highlighted his perspective on marketing and the modern ways that were now becoming a necessity for the present and future marketplace. I interviewed him immediately, despite having no vacancies. I was simply intrigued. In the interview, everything he said put the training course, run by the Software Company, into context. So, it hadn't been a load of rubbish (I never said that!). Instead, the course was based on techniques that this guy, who was less than half my age, was highlighting as being quite effective.

He was from another industry, but, what the hell, why not? Something different. It was a great decision indeed.

I needed to accept that, although I completed a marketing course (okay, okay, it was 25 years ago!), my techniques and methods were rapidly becoming outdated. The younger generation were now more relevant than ever.

I noticed this with Sales Directors and other Group Boards, too. I'd often been told that sales and marketing worked better together, with Sales Directors craving the extra responsibility and Group Boards believing that marketing was there to support sales.

I can safely say that, in many organisations, marketing is viewed as the admin side of sales. Well, there you go, failure is assured.

Neither, in my opinion, are slaves to the other. Marketing needs to be its own function, with its own up to date expertise, with sales being the follow up to the marketing messages and nurturing process.

Marketing therefore needs to be understood and given its own board seat so it can set the pace for opportunities, not just play the role of administration for sales.

I am sure that there are Sales Directors out there who love marketing, and this is good for business. Although, when times are tough, where do they go to hide (you know where this is going)? Yep, marketing. The role of a combined functional sales and marketing role can be effective, or not. It all depends on the structure in place. A large organisation may have a Sales and Marketing Director who is very hands off, leaving each teams' sub functions to become experts in their own field. Naturally, though, this can still work well.

On the other hand, there are many Sales Directors who live to take over marketing and control the messages that are pushed out there. So, is this power and politics, or genuine desire? It could be either. Going back to the start of this section, we must ask the question as to whether the Sales Director is up to date with current marketing strategies. If not, it's likely you will lose your marketing teams' expertise to a person who will not bring out the best from them. In this instance, they will become a bunch of glorified sales administrators.

I once saw this after recruiting some great, energetic and current marketing people. During my three week absence, the Sales Director, who was a major force in the Company, ran a customer event. He decided to make sure that the team were kept busy, and bypassed the Marketing Director, using his 'authority' as leverage.

Upon my return, I found out that the team had acted as hosts to customers, meeting and greeting them, offering hospitality, serving food and valet parking vehicles for guests. They had also washed and tidied up after the event.

This totally un-called for happening was led by a person who did not have his own team. And I understood why that was the case, and thank goodness that he didn't. After some time, I reassured all involved that this was not something that would happen again. Eventually, we all learnt to love each other once more.

From the team's perspective, it was obvious that their expertise had not been recognised. By occupying a seat in the office each day while the sales team were 'on the road', they were seen as the ones left behind to do general admin. I'm pleased to say that this was not a view I supported.

The **Third** example are Leaders who tend to combine roles to save money. In the process, they place marketing somewhere and anywhere (as they do not know what to do with it, just like training), whereby it then can be viewed as a support to sales or to carry out admin functions. In this position, it loses credibility and is dragged down by sales not driving it as they should. If not understood, at some point, it will fall apart by losing its great and unique talent, something that will be hard to replace.

Therefore, it has always been my preference to separate these functions from each other. Marketing should sit with someone who has passion and current awareness of this specialism. If in doubt, I would hire an interim, or part-time person with the right credentials.

Saving money on marketing promotes a false sense of security. Likewise, taking on a good administrator on a full-time basis is beneficial. Although, it will not address the lack of marketing experience that may be required.

As a Leader, being able to recognise talent, and talent gaps, is central to the role, something that can be supported through the provision of Psychometric tests (conducted by an expert, of course, not some crazy enthusiast). It would demonstrate to other internal colleagues why 'Joanna' was different to the others. It also helps people recognise why a balanced set of skills is essential, as well as helping them grasp the concept of unique characters and, importantly, why we need them.

After all, it would certainly be a boring world if we were all the same.

CLIENTS – A LOVE/HATE RELATIONSHIP

In my leasing days, I was part of a selling team. As we went through the due diligence process with a potential new owner, the Divisional MD of the buyer said, 'We love our clients for ever. Do you?' Well, I knew what the right answer was, based on their views, but what was I to say. Well, honesty is the best policy and all that, and so I told them what I thought (I was opinionated even in those days!).

No, was my reply, I do not love our customers for ever. In fact, I truly hate some of our customers. I detest them. Some of them, I actually loathe!

The distaste on the Divisional MD's face was akin to me spitting in front of him. His disbelief was palpable. It was clear that he thought my attitude towards customers was not a good attribute to have. Reluctantly, through gritted teeth, he asked me why?

Well, we have clients who pay for X and then want X+1 without paying for the +1. Then we have clients who attempt to use unpaid invoices to lever more of our services free of charge before paying what they owed for services commissioned and delivered. Often with services delivered several months prior. I have since seen similar scenarios in other industries, and this behaviour has only increased over the last decade.

We had one client (a household brand), who ran up an unpaid bill of £125k for services we had supplied. To make matters worse, just for the hell of it, the client offered us 19%, as they claimed they were 100 times bigger than us. Also, following delivery of the vehicles, they claimed that they were not happy with the service (they hadn't complained when we were working on their deliverables).

So, do we love our customers? Definitely not all of them forever. Don't get me wrong, there were some clients we had loved working with. And so the Divisional MD's ignorance continued. According to him, his Company loved all clients for ever. He needed to know we were in-line with his viewpoint and were on-board. I'm not sure whether this was a question, a request, a demand or an ultimatum. Whatever it was, I did not sit on the fence. I gladly highlighted that anyone who loves these types of clients would be an idiot. That was it. I had surely sealed my next career move, which would be out of the door upon sale of the Company. But, surely, he could not have been of sane mind? How can anyone love clients for ever so blindly? Especially considering the fact that I was in a National Accounts role at the time, which was very client centric.

It was a romantic thought at best, and not at all practical for an MD of a large organisation. In my opinion, this is typically the view a naïve sales person would need to adopt, focusing on long-term relationships regardless of the commercial benefit to both sides.

Similarly, in my Software days, I would often ask our software developers, and the sales people, whether they enjoyed working with certain client organisations. Invariably, the response was positive, after all they were creating excellent technical solutions and generating invoices. But what about the bit that went wrong, the bit where the client failed to settle the invoice? It always felt like this was a parallel universe, existing only for the negative. Existing for those who thrived on problems, those who wanted to find that glass half empty all the time. However, when I merged the two sides together ... what a reaction I got!

When I informed the sales person that no payment from the client meant recovery of their commission payment received for the sale three months ago ... well, ouch.

When I informed the technical wizards that their great creativity in helping the client achieve something remarkable using software was felt to be not worthy of payment ... oh dear.

We then started to reveal the impact of the client not paying with our teams, the common question was: why would they not pay us?

There was a time when I took the helm of the Company as its Director. It was a good solid business that historically ran on sound principles, trust and integrity.

The Company had a flagship client, which was certainly not the biggest client we had by any stretch. But it was a client we loved at the time. Well, they say that love is blind … yes, I was soon to be reminded of this.

Our client, who really understood the value of what we did, knew that any investment they made with us was the way to differentiate their service. They knew it was a way of growing output without pro-rated investment in headcount. They genuinely valued our services. For many years, they talked about a multi-million investment with us – wow, we really loved this client. A marriage and future offspring didn't sound too bad (you get my thinking).

Two years into my role, I met with the client and asked them the question no one else had: when are you going to move on this investment you keep on talking about it? On a gratis basis, we had freely shared idea after idea, solution after solution. In return, and in all fairness to the client, they had offered a reference or two for the free consulting we had given them over the course of time. Their response to my rather bold question concerned me, so I pushed this as far as I could. After all, my Shareholders were only thinking what I was asking: when would we get this return on investment? Long before I joined, and every day since, we had been supplying technical documents, as well as ideas and suggestions on developing their service, based on our many years of experience.

The client's response was, 'I recognise your anxiety and thank you for your Company's help to date. I can assure you that this will be going ahead shortly.' My abruptness had given me what I had hoped for. This was close, was it not?

Our Sales Director continued to entertain the client, supplying details and information to them for several weeks after. One night, I received a text from my Sales Director, after they'd spent the evening entertaining with this client.

The text read: 'I cannot believe the news. They [the client] informed me that, two weeks ago, they commenced the project with another supplier.'

So, all the while we were entertaining this client, they had been deliberately misleading us. They had lied to us at the expense of us feeding and watering them!

I calmly spoke to the client the next day. They said, 'I did not lie to you. I confirmed the project was going ahead, and it was … I just omitted to tell you it was with another supplier.' I did tell the client what I thought of this tactic and, needless to say, we did not do much business together again. Note the words 'not much'. Why not 'none at all'?

Well, some poetic justice came of this. The client was so busy revelling in their conquest over us, he forgot to terminate his support contract, which automatically renewed at £60k per annum. Realising his error, he asked for our support to rectify this obvious oversight. He wouldn't, of course, be able to justify this to his board, especially as he had signed for support with the new supplier. There was no way he could pay us as well. As you would expect, my professionalism kicked in and our response was appropriate and supportive – well, no, not really. I made sure he paid that bloody invoice and I laughed my head off.

So, forgive me when I say that I cannot adopt a policy of love all clients for ever. There are two variables here, and things change over time, as so do clients' attitudes when it comes to greed. Over the many years I have spent in the business world, I still see such practices continue.

Despite sounding rather negative, I have found some clients who have become lifelong friends. Although, I think these things are formed on mutually acceptable terms and respect for one another.

Often that respect is earned by recognising that you need each other. You need to help each other and making sure that the other party can survive and evolve without wanting to pursue a one-sided agenda at any cost.

SHOW ME THE MONEY

Any Director will recognise the need to take risks as a necessary step towards reaping rewards at a later stage.

A business that is failing, though, may not have the luxury of time to sit back and wait for income to catch up with outgoings in the same way a profitable business may have.

If your teams are properly engaged and understand the challenges that lie ahead, they might be more accepting of a change of reward strategy in favour of the long-term gain of retaining their jobs and stability of the Company.

This is likely to be in the form of not getting a pay increase for a few years. A service business can be heavy on staff costs and, therefore, a Retail Price Index (RPI) increase or similar can be the difference between staying afloat and going under.

I have needed to deploy this strategy out of necessity, although, I would also recommend this in a profitable business. Let me explain before the squishy tomatoes get thrown at me again.

Many British companies have, for many years, taken a view that RPI or inflationary increase is given as a flat rate to all staff as a fair reward based on the cost of living increasing.

In more recent times, more and more Companies have adopted a variant to this thinking. They keep the same overall increase, say 2.5% for example, but give some staff 4% and others 1%, provided the overall expense is within budget.

This is a great approach, as those who work hardest or more effectively should get recognised separately to those who are happy to turn up every day and just do what is asked of them.

I am not trying to decree the consistent, hard-working person who is happy just doing what they need to. All businesses have these people and they play a vital role. I am, however, saying that some people deserve more than others in each review period, based on their contributions or effort. To those who push themselves beyond the everyday, it would be de-motivating to receive the same rewards as those who did not.

This is a common reason for people leaving. It is not just the pay, but the principle that their efforts are not recognised.

Let's now take this a step further and be a little more controversial (who me?).

Imagine a working culture where there isn't a salary rise – ever.

The salary increase budget is still agreed by the board and in place. Let's say it's 2.5% of total salary costs. Rather than the awkwardness of the annual appraisal, where manager and staff sit and reminisce over achievements, let's replace it with a monthly 1-2-1 meeting.

In the meeting, issues are raised on both sides, praise is given and objectives are set for the next month, documented and shared.

Then, add in a self-scoring mechanism to be discussed with the person's manager. The self-scoring methodology is simple and awards points for doing a good job (as expected), for going the extra mile and/or for bringing in innovation or creativity. Naturally, the scores can also reflect below par performance too. A reward is discussed following three months of consistent, good performance. The reward is likely to be something worthwhile and meaningful, rather than the typical 2.5% of an average salary. I suggest something more like a £2,000 increase each time rather than £350 per year.

This way, staff know they can be rewarded at any time, rather than having to wait until the last-minute surge before year end. It helps for them to also realise that the harder they work, the greater the reward.

Naturally, you reward the best performers. Typically, this can (if managed correctly) stimulate huge motivation with less of a budget impact, as the funds would simply shift from those underperforming.

People need to know what they must do to go the extra mile. Give them stretched objectives. Some people will impress and achieve greater rewards, and others will not quite get there. The latter will recognise that a pay increase is unlikely, taking the awkwardness away from the inevitable conversation.

Also by setting objectives and incentivising initiatives, people are empowered as they are in charge of their own rewards, which is self-funded by excellent achievements and innovation.

If one person does a super job, and continues to impress several times a year, reward them accordingly. This will energise them. Others will become aware of this happening, so show them, hold these achievers up as examples of how to get more out of the Company.

Obviously, as more and more people rise to the same level, you can be more selective, raise the bar or even stretch the boundaries to suit.

Perhaps a little controversial, but why reward everyone the same way? People are not the same, they do not perform the same and they do not want to be treated the same.

So, when your next team member knocks on your door asking for an increase, revisit their monthly 1-2-1 notes. See what they have achieved and what have they done to make a difference. Those who do more, should be rewarded more.

When they know this, your answer need not be 'sorry, I cannot help' but, 'yes, of course. Would love to help. What do you feel you can do differently in the next few months that will help the Company?'. When these two things align, both parties are happy. Inevitably, not everyone will be able to raise their game, and they, then, are responsible for not getting more. Management override is always a good thing in these circumstances. Particularly in cases where you need to make a special case to retain their motivation with softer objectives or easy to reach goals.

When people are aware that no automatic pay rises are awarded unless one works hard, the usual feeling of entitlement is replaced with one of feeling rather special – the way it should be. They have earned it.

Unless you really need to, why pay more to staff each year when they do not contribute more?

As a slight angle on this, there was a time in my recruitment days when one person complained about not getting a pay increase for two years. We went through the same scenario as above, and, although she understood it, she felt the need to continue pushing for a pay rise. Pride, embarrassment or genuine belief, maybe?

An unfortunate event then occurred, her mother was hospitalised. As a conscientious member of staff, she did her job by day, and spent her nights at the hospital.

I asked her manager to give her a week of afternoons off, so that she could get to the hospital earlier. Her manager questioned whether this was a good idea as she had become a little rebellious recently. So, why would we help her?

It was a good question, but I do not think her demands were all about money. She was reasonably comfortable in financial terms (something I knew from talking to her on many occasions). I recognised that all she wanted was to feel valued, and a pay increase was her only known path to recognising her value. This is likely to be the case with other people.

Naturally, she was appreciative of the time given to her. But a few days later, she asked to see me with her manager. She apologised for her outburst over salary, highlighting that her performance was not as good as it could have been over recent months and that she understood my decision over her salary, which she did not want to push anymore. Her mother had been unwell for months, and this had created a level of insecurity for her, which she felt could be addressed through a financial boost. Seeing how we reacted to her compassionate needs, her loyalty, performance and happiness returned instantly. She had recognised that, regardless of financial awards, she had been treated better than she could have expected. This gave her the feeling of security and value at a time when she needed it.

In the same way, she became a strong advocate to the process or meritocracy after achieving her own financial recognition based on great performance.

The ones who excel, will love it. Those who plod along will not be happy. But, you will find that, in time, they themselves will impress and recognise that it is not all bad after all.

Additionally, it is important to recognise other things that hold value to your people beyond a salary.

We must, however, also recognise that some people will have a genuine need for more money, not just a desire. Management override for a pay increase will, at times, be essential.

I recall a recent event where I granted a Company loan (in line with HMRC rules, of course) to a staff member.

He was a brilliant young chap who was destined for greatness, although he had only been with us for a year. He was on a less than average salary, was doing a great job and was due to receive an increase shortly based on his efforts to date.

He approached his manager and mentioned that he'd been offered another job. He was happy with the Company and the role and was somehow saddened to leave, but he needed the money.

Having got married some time before, he was desperately trying to take on financial responsibility. In doing so, he opened up (after my stealth questioning, of course) and explained that he had used up his limit on his credit cards which was £8,000. The interest on his monthly payment (and he was not clearing the balance) was sufficient to make him seek a role offering more money as he was genuinely struggling.

We had trained him well and he held massive value to us. He had been offered a £9,000 per year increase and showed us the offer. For us to replace him via an agency, it would have cost £7,000 (20% of his £35k salary).

I offered him an interest free, tax free loan of £8,000, which cleared his cards and allowed him to make repayments over three years, with no interest to contend with.

His salary increased in time, although not straight away. He stayed with the Company for two reasons.

1. His immediate needs were addressed in a unique way
2. He knew that we needed him and were prepared to take a risk in helping him

My Shareholders questioned my methods. Although the loyalty, hard work and commitment from this person was incredible, the risk, of course, was still there, but manageable.

Since then, wherever possible, I have continued to offer staff loans in this way as I recognise that everyone has a reason for coming to work beyond making the Leader successful.

THE PAPER MOUNTAIN

One of my employers, a major Global manufacturer, once offered a time management course. I was looking forward to it. It was a two-day session on site, with lunch, which was always delightful. Essentially, it meant a two-day break from working. Happy days when you are 23-years-old.

I then found out that my boss, who was an unlikely manager himself, was also attending the very same course. He was an accomplished Ox-bridge graduate, hence his managerial role. This Company favoured people from certain educational backgrounds. Was he purposefully trying to ruin my two-day break?

At the age of 23, anyone attending an in-house course with their colleagues will quickly relate to the feeling of the introductions being like a classroom-based 'Facebook' event, where socialising is the goal. Being educated comes a far second by comparison.

Then, the course tutor arrived. He was not someone from the training department, but a tall imposing character. He had stern look about him, and was certainly in no mood to make friends, nor was he happy for anyone else to do so either.

Even my boss looked terrified. The tutor settled everyone, not with words, but with a glare. It was a blank, distant stare that was focused on something, seemingly, a thousand miles beyond the conference room wall.

Silence fell. Moments seemed like an age as we looked at each other for comfort and familiarity.

He introduced himself. Rather than using words as normal people do, he stated his name and details of his background whilst stomping and marching. Oh shit, a military man. A man of rules and strictness. He was an officer in the grenadier guards turned trainer, just so he could discipline us all, with, no doubt, the odd bit of humiliation for good measure.

No way was he getting me up and marching like a soldier. If I wanted to join the army and be a target, I would have joined (not that I would have been accepted due to attitude and poor fitness).

With all this stomping and establishment, we still ended up with a rather good course.

I recall him choosing to use me as an example to the rest of the group (probably because I was a little outspoken and he was trying to deal with my unruliness). At the time, though, I had different views.

He asked me to take a piece of paper for each task I currently had on my desk. This was before email was widely used.

While he continued with his speech to the group, I was working in the background, creating a new piece of A4 for each task, writing only the headline on each page (a complete waste of paper, although I assumed he knew what he was doing).

By the time I had finished, there was stack of papers. He'd chose the wrong guy to pick on that day. My boss was sitting there and I was determined to showcase just how much work I had to do. The pile of paper was mountainous, but there was no reaction from the tutor, as though my pile was unimpressive. Surely not. He was just trying to ignore how impressive this was.

He then called me over to stand next to him. His hand rested on my shoulder, while one finger tapped my jacket to make sure everyone focused on his hand as he spoke. The gesture was somehow disturbing and intimidating.

He did, indeed, take the time to recognise the enormity of the workload I had. He asked me to prioritise these in order. I cheekily responded to say that they all needed urgent attention and 'were all important'. This made me feel quite important, too. After all, my work is important, I am in demand and people relied on me.

My response prompted a reaction, one that left me speechless and rather confused. He took my pile of paper, removed one piece and put the rest in the bin. In the bloody bin!

Yes, this was the humiliation I was expecting. I had not known in what form or shape it would come, but I knew he would do something like this.

The other delegates laughed as he took the remaining sheet of paper and made sure it went into the metal bucket. He forced it in with his large hands while not even cracking a smile, despite my colleagues and my boss now really enjoying this for the first time. My boss was revelling in this fun, no doubt glad that I was the one picked on for this humiliating lesson, rather than him. Okay, self-preservation, I get it. I would no doubt have been the same.

He proceeded with his messages whilst I stood there being observed by the others. My embarrassment was increasing and I was now starting to get a little angry. He was mocking me. Any credibility I had over the next two days was to be trashed. It was not the start to the day I had hoped for at all.

Suddenly, he started to make sense. Referring to my mountain of paper, he asked how one could be expected to deal with all this work in one go. Hence why he took out one piece and binned the rest. Quite right, I thought.

He asked me to list out the other tasks, summarising it all, but not in detail. He wanted to know whether I could recall them.

This was easy as I had just listed each task on a piece of paper.

He went on to ask what would happen if I failed to deliver the work expected of me. Looking at my boss, I responded politely. I said that I would probably receive a call to remind me of outstanding tasks, and they'd give me a response deadline.

He used this as a way of setting the scene for the time management course: learning the art of prioritising.

I sat down, but before I did, I looked at my boss. It seemed like he was starting to feel less smug and was notably concerned about the lesson of putting the bulk of my work in the bin while concentrating on doing one thing well at a time. Essentially, removing any clutter from my in-tray and, in doing so, removing clutter from my mind.

Could this be real? Permission to bin my workload? Awesome course. I could not wait for the second day. Maybe I'd get permission to have a lay in until 9 a.m. Though, even I knew this would be pushing it.

The point of day one was that, looking at a mountain of paper was an impossible task when trying to feel on top of your job. Inevitably, the harder jobs got left behind, growing with the mountain. The mountain would be visible to all, who, in turn, would also stress over it, fixate on the problem and not see any achievement. Crikey, no wonder I hated my job at times.

We then went on to make our own lists on one page. We discussed amongst one another, including with our managers, to decide what was deemed a priority and, more importantly, why.

So, this was easy. First in, first out, then? Not so. We were asked to re-work this list, daily. Surely this was adding to my work, not reducing it!

Re-prioritising daily actually made things a little more enjoyable than just staring at a pile of paper. And what of the pile of paper? Well, I would not put it in the bin. Instead, I would keep it out of sight, somewhere I could find it easily enough.

Shockingly, though, it worked. It is a system I have maintained for 26 years. Okay, technology has made life easier, through allowing people to access information faster, more immediately, but this just reinforces the need to prioritise. It is now more important than ever, as people expect immediate responses.

Checking things off a list is really empowering. It demonstrates achievement each day and ensures nothing important gets buried in the mountain. It enables one to stay on top of the job, rather than get bogged down in a paper mountain.

The list was designed to include all aspects of one's life, rather than separate work and personal lists. One summary of everything on your mind works better. It helps you prioritise and de-stresses your mind as you are clear on your achievements and outstanding tasks.

I often remind myself of this course and the lessons I learnt, as taught by this imposing military officer; a person I will never forget.

GROW YOUR
OWN TALENT

Everyone wants the best people and the recruitment process is fundamental to this. After all, this decision reflects on you personally, and taking the time to get it right is important.

In an internet-age, where people demand immediate responses, taking too much time can leave you with second best.

I find it amazing that companies get this wrong so often. They place multiple hurdles in place, dragging the candidates through their many steps of evaluation.

I am not against putting a candidate through a tough interview or two. Especially as I am not known for being a pleasant conversationalist during these meetings. But I am focused.

All too often, the interviewers get absorbed with finding the perfect match with the job description. Focusing on the reasons why a person cannot do the job justifying a Companies hesitation.

How often do you look at your job description during an interview, only to find that you have everything, absolutely everything the role requires, there? If you do, congratulations. I wish you happiness in your life of boredom.

Life often involves compromise. I have yet to meet a person who matches a job description and person specification in completeness. And I never expect to.

So, what can we really expect? Well, it's reasonable to expect candidates to have the pre-requisite skills or experiences required to do a reasonably good job.

The interview should focus on testing the validity of their application. Equally important is to ensure their character fits, whether they want this and why.

I always look for attitude. Qualifications are no indication of whether someone will try hard to do what is expected. I have never fired anyone for lack of skills, that's why we have training courses. If this fails, then look in the mirror: look at your Leadership or management style to see where it is failing. Someone who wants to do the job well, will do so, provided they have good Leadership and the right support tools.

When I left school, I remember writing to 50 organisations, picking them from the telephone directory. I knew nothing of recruitment agencies or the correct protocol for finding a job.

In 1983, at 16, it was common place to write a letter, then wait around 28 days to get a response. Today, a lack of response within a few days or even hours would not be welcome. So, times have indeed changed. Impatience is our way of life and immediacy is now a requirement of society, thanks to the birth of the internet.

This is not a moan about the good old days. Far from it. I really do love the immediacy the internet brings us, and I am a proud early adopter of technology for my age group as I am rather impatient myself.

Yet, when it comes to hiring someone, we are often stuck with the attitude we had in the 80s and 90s when making decisions. Our candidates expect a more immediate response.

An outsourcing Company I once worked for had a great process for everything. Recruiting staff had a five-meeting process put in place by an experienced HR Director.

I took part in this process as a hiring manager (Functional Director). I was in awe of this excellent process from an outsourcing Company – we were determined to find the best candidate.

The process that followed did give us the excellent internal engagement we desired.

The process consisted of five stages, but after the first stage meeting, I knew I had a preference for one candidate. He desired it more than any of the others. We got on well and trust was established. He did not have the best CV, yet, my thoughts were cemented.

Four meetings and five weeks later, the candidate found another job – oh dear, that was a shame. I really wanted him.

No bother. We had many candidates. After meeting five, and nearly six weeks later, we were ready for a decision. However, the second preferred candidate opted out of the process for another offer. What the hell was happening to these candidates?

Well, we eventually hired someone. They fit the criteria and job description quite well. Three weeks later, he accepted another position that offered more money, and subsequently left.

'People eh', was the message shared internally. Yes, people; **us** not the candidates. We were looking for the best, but who or what was the best?

The best for me was someone who really wanted the job, and could do it. Well, we established that all candidates could do the job in the main. Although, the one I wanted could not hang on indefinitely. And why should he? We offered no certainty, there was no job offer, just more meetings. A bit like The X Factor auditions, but without the captivity or singing!

To the candidate, this must have seemed like, 'We are still unsure about you.' How else could this be interpreted?

I wonder how this would work for us in our personal lives. As crude as it will sound, people do not like having opportunities dangled in front of them, without getting it (the opportunity that is ... get your minds out of the gutter!). If we dated a person we liked, but kept saying I might want a relationship with you, but I am considering a few others too until I can be sure, would we ever be happy with that? We often know what we want quickly, and life often requires some compromise. It is quite common to seek perfection in our personal relationships, although we put aside any imperfections as we recognise that no-one is perfect. Finding that spark, that something special, that mutual desire is all that is necessary for a relationship to continue, consider marriage or start a family.

So, why is recruiting the right person so hard? Do we fail to trust our instincts? Perhaps we are too busy trying to impress, and in the process, we fail to do what is instinctive.

The point here is that no-one is perfect. People change and move on. We rarely have them for ever. So, surely then, it is worth taking a risk, making that decision on someone, imperfections and all, to give them a chance?

I am not suggesting we give the job to the first person we meet because it is easier, that would be wrong. I mean, make a decision based on what you feel.

Whenever I interview for a specific position, I always invite the candidates for interview within three days of each other. I would never drag the process out. It would be unfair on the first candidate as they'd be left hanging on unfairly to receive feedback.

Each candidate will possess a reasonable level of skill to undertake most of the job. From my perspective, I am looking at the things I referred to above: the spark, the desire and the feeling of trust.

My interviews always consist of awkward questions, but not in a nasty, aggressive way. I just want to get what I want as quickly as is practically possible. I always dedicate a portion of the meeting to finding out what the candidate wants to know or have clarified before accepting a position. It also helps determine whether they have truly thought the position through, or whether this is just another job to them. Taking another job is also fine, if their motives to work are strong. Although, recruiting a new member of the team must be a two-way thing, just like finding a partner to share our lives with.

Rarely do we get this right every time. So, why waste time and lose the people we want by taking too long? I am sure there are many reasons, yet it does not guarantee better results.

Hiring managers are often not empowered by their Leaders to make decisions. As a hiring manager, you must ask yourself whether (with your help) this person can grow in this role? We often create our own obstacles in life; the hiring process is no different.

As humans, many of us are programmed to sit tight, follow protocols and wait for instructions. If such things are pre-programmed, is it the individual's fault? I do not think so.

The role of the Leader, in this context, is to support others as they take a step into the unknown, to help give them the confidence to trust themselves and their own abilities and to make decisions based on their feelings. Our people still need direction.

Some of the Leaders I have met over the past years talk about empowerment like they get it. Unless you practice it, stand by it and actively help your team develop it, you don't get it at all.

Instead, it just becomes a blame culture (a Teflon Ron moment). 'You did it, and on your head be it.' Well, that's a sure way of breeding sheep, not the next generation of Leaders.

I remember a manager (who I reported to), from my fleet management days, who spoke to me about a decision that needed to be made regarding one of our clients.

He asked me what I would do if I were him. I remember thinking, 'Ah, I see what you are doing. You want me to make the decision and then blame me if it goes wrong'… after all, his Director was nicknamed Teflon Ron for a reason, and we all know that Teflon is non-stick!

He supported my suggestion and confirmed that I could go ahead with my idea. It worked, of course. I knew it was a good idea. It was mine after all!

From then onwards, we talked about new ideas, my ideas. I had a forum for putting my views into practice.

He often backed my suggestions (not all of them I know, but many of them). The caveat of his support reduced in time, and I grew in confidence. But, guess what, I also grew in seniority. I had become empowered to make decisions, and was responsible for the outcomes.

Eventually, I asked the manager, who became the Director why he was crazy enough to trust a minion such as myself, considering my lack of experience and track record. From his perspective, he said, my energy, my passion and my desire to try new things were obviously for the benefit of the Company. Consequently, with each opportunity, he let me go further and take more and more responsibility, until I reached a point where I could not remember a life without empowerment.

So, back to the point of recruiting. Candidates are people who want to feel wanted and loved for the things that make them unique and special. Finding fault with gaps in their CV is easy, matching the CV to the job description is never going to be exact, so rejecting a candidate could simply be down to the fact that someone wants to feel a sense of self-importance.

Taking six weeks to hire someone will either exhaust them or energise them. Just think how you would feel if someone was prepared to overlook your inexperience because they loved other things about you. This is something not all managers can do, but the experience can truly make you feel fantastic.

After selling a business, I remember not needing to earn the big bucks I did in my lucrative past. I saw a position for a CEO based near my home. It was for a charity and the salary was low. But I was energised for the position as the charity was close to my personal circumstances.

The position stated that, due to concerns over long-term funding for their cause, they needed someone to start immediately, and, to top all of this, it was only a six month contract.

I applied to the agency that was working on this exclusive vacancy. They were looking for someone who had my experience, although I had not worked with a charity before.

The agency informed me that my application was not successful. The charity wanted someone with charity experience. Really? Okay, well you cannot win them all I guess.

Three months later, the same agency was still advertising this vacancy. Knowing how agencies work, I just assumed they were advertising this role to drive candidates to their website, despite the vacancy being filled. I was discussing another role with the agency when I asked, out of curiosity, what had happened to the CEO role with the charity. They informed me that the charity was struggling to fill the role as their trustees could not decide on a candidate who met their profile 100%. They had a candidate who was a good fit, but after two months of meetings, they'd lost the candidate to another position. The candidate had obviously felt unwanted by this charity and, quite rightly, wandered away elsewhere. I know where I would work, and it wasn't with this charity.

So, wanting the best person for the job involves much more than words, or a good brand. Take time to make people feel appreciated for the skills they have. Everyone has something special. It is up to us as Leaders to spot this and find out how we can best use this to our advantage. Thereby, securing the candidate swiftly and not making them feel they were further down the list of choices. It's important for the candidate to know that we want them specifically, not just any candidate. After all, as employers, we want a candidate to want us and not just any old job.

IF IN DOUBT – 'DO NOWT'

As a business Leader, there is a steady stream of decisions your staff and board need or want you to make. With these decisions comes the rap if things go wrong.

I have always prided myself on being a decisive person. Whether it's a 'yes' or 'no', you will invariably upset someone: a colleague or your board. Can you win?

Well, there is a third option, which a previous CEO of mine told me about. That third option is to simply do nothing, yet.

It may sound strange, but it can be a useful option. People who knock on your door as a business Leader, like to have your support. Not only is this beneficial for their political standing, it can be beneficial to the Company; telling the difference, if one exists, is difficult.

This CEO told me that, unless a decision was necessary, he would not respond with a 'yes' or 'no' answer immediately. He would push back and wait for a compelling reason to prioritise, address and decide. In the meantime, he parked it (the Burning Platform again).

This dilemma presented itself recently, just before I sold the business I was running.

We had Intellectual Property (IP) rights in a product that was produced several years before I joined the Company.

Essentially, the IP was developed for a potential market in the UK, which never came to fruition. By the time I joined, several other attempts had been made to sell this in the UK (all failed). By this point in time, the product had become outdated as it ran on a software platform that was no longer available or supported.

Our sales team and Shareholders wanted to invest in modernising the product, which would need upgrading every couple of years to stay abreast with technical advances. There was a market out there, but in other regions of the world, potentially Africa and the Far East.

The investment in the product without new sales would cost the Company 20% of their profits in the first year. So, an easy decision of 'no' then?

Not really. When faced with compelling arguments, such as the sales team saying they could demo the modernised product and sell it, it does stand a chance.

Shareholders argued that there was value in the IP and that potential investors/new owners would value highly.

To shut down further investment into upgrading the product would not be the right approach. I was seen as being obstructive, a killer of a sales opportunity, ignorant to new markets and lacking vision and innovation. This then spread to the technical team, marketing and support. It would have been seen as a stand against the Shareholders, whose money paid my wages, whose interests I represented.

My concern, of course, was the reduction in profit by 20% over the next year. There would be a side impact: immediate job security, team bonuses and, of course, the question of, what if?

What if the sales team could not sell it in two years? Twelve months later, we would need to consider modernising it again.

What if after the investment was made, the sales team generated an opportunity where further changes or modifications were required, which were things we could not charge for? (a common issue in this product sector).

Naturally, if the Shareholders had told me not to worry about a 20% dip in profits, then I would have had some support. As it stood, we were on a mission to sell the Company, therefore, maximising every penny of profit was essential. Although, this is typically important for all Companies at all times. Also, when considering a sale, it would be valuable to maximise the value of 'Good Will', something the investment in IP would have given us. So, what were we to do?

Over the next two years, I did nothing other than stay on top of the options available to me. I stayed up to date with my team's views, market forces, including client views, and industry needs.

It is a scary prospect when a Leader must walk down a path that splits left or right, knowing there is impending doom either way. It is a fear akin to going down a path of no return, potentially a dangerous journey that could stain your unblemished career.

Refusing to try or backing out reduces your teams' respect for you. After all, they expect the Leader to make a decision with the CEO's stamp of approval, especially given the risks.

I did decide, which I then shared with my teams.

I announced that we would invest in this product at the right time. The right time would be when we had a client who was willing to pay for it. Or, if the potential buyer for the Company dictated it must be updated before the sale was completed.

It was my responsibility to promote this concept to a new buyer, with the support of the sales team, who would be responsible for asking clients to pay more to cover the product's update.

My credibility was on the ropes. I was taking punches from all directions. Although, that night, I slept well.

The sales team were pushing back. They wanted me to make their job easier by providing a finished product to sell, rather than some pioneering sales development. I've seen other companies do this, especially with start-up technology, and they were successful.

The Shareholders would still hold me to ransom over poor performance. I had to be sure I had confidence in the sales team to promote it, otherwise profits would drop unnecessarily. This way, staff would retain security, we'd keep our jobs … a good day's work.

Three years following the decision to upgrade the product, the Company was sold. The buyers insisted that we update the product in line with market trends, which had recently changed. The technology platform had also improved over this period; so much less work was required to upgrade this IP.

So, essentially, by deciding to do nothing 'yet', we preserved jobs, profitability and, ultimately, the share sale price of the Company. Upgrading the product only happened when there was a compelling need for it.

Had I given in to the pressure from my teams and Shareholders, I am not sure there would have been as positive an outcome.

Conversely though, I do admire decision-makers, especially being one myself. Seek out the compelling reason – the Burning Platform.

When you create your team of Directors, at times you will see a wave of decisions being processed. This is when a string of 'no' decisions are made: no to new initiatives, no to investment, no to recruiting incremental headcount or, no to a change in process.

Be aware – why?

Confidence.

Imagine a person in a loss-making environment, their business division or department is likely to be under enormous pressure to perform and deliver its product or service.

In this situation, there's bound to be a wide range of ideas from their teams. The easiest way out in this case, is to say no. By doing this, the response ensures no accountability for the new initiative, no neck on the block, allowing one to just plod on.

This is expected of a functional team leader, not a change maker. In itself, there is nothing wrong with this approach and, to be honest, many new initiatives receive a short response of 'no thanks'.

Earlier, we talked about finding reasons not to hire someone as there is rarely a perfect fit with the job specification document. New initiatives have similar outcomes.

It is common to look for the problem: what if something goes wrong? Something new will have my name on it and I will need to take ownership. Oh dear, my personal credibility! Perhaps it's safer to sit tight in ignorance.

So, watch out for the decision-maker who is always ready to say 'no'. In reality, this is not a true decision-maker, they are weak Leaders. Weak Leaders do their best to avoid confrontation of the issues, lack accountability and seek out the easy route, which often does not exist.

EXCUSE ME –
CAN I HAVE A SAY?

A good Leader will have generated the time to explore new ideas with their teams. The teams, led by their Directors or Functional Heads, will be expected to initiate ideas for change, for betterment and growth. In my opinion, such engagement is an excellent way forward. It demonstrates a culture of democratic thinking and decision-making, provided, of course, everyone contributes. If not, you end up with the strongest voices getting their two pence worth in, while others sit idle, thinking about their day jobs.

I was recently asked to help a local Company looking at change. They wanted someone to support the owner (MD) in creating new ideas and initiatives.

He talked to me about his team of managers, none of whom had been given freedom of speech or authority. He was, by his own admission, the Director of this £10m family-owned business.

He outlined his management meeting style, which seemed to revolve around reporting to him in front of others, not working together as equals. Clearly, they need a book like this, I thought. Although, the daily rate for my services at the time was far more lucrative.

He was quite concerned about how to change this culture. Other than the Financial Controller, no one really had any views or ideas, especially as discussions were rare (if you disregard their monthly updates).

The Company was successful. Being a well-known local brand and supplier of goods to the trade, it was financially sound and led by a successful owner.

So, my attention turned to him.

My priority was to find out more about the management meetings, so I offered to sit in in one of them, just as an observer. Understandably, he was reluctant to grant this request. In some ways, it was almost as though I was judging him, forming a critique and searching for ways to change him.

I persisted, and he eventually agreed. Probably more out of curiosity rather than anything else. I kept my word and sat in as an observer, allowing him to 'maintain control'.

One thing was immediately obvious. He spoke for everyone. He dished out the bollockings, the praise and basically controlled every point of conversation.

In my opinion, he was a decent, likeable chap (we have known each other for some time), and the Company was thriving under him. Following the meeting, he asked for feedback. He wanted to know how he could engage with and encourage people to participate, be more proactive and more forthcoming with ideas.

As a middle-aged Sagittarian, I am known for my directness. I shared my observations as kindly as I could without hurting his feelings. He agreed that he was dominant and needed to be so as the team were not strong. Dominating was his way of compensating for what his team lacked. Okay, I recognise the self-preservation point. It was true that none of them were engaged or forthcoming with ideas or suggestions for betterment, but equally, they did not want to be there as they got the same old shit each month.

'So, how do I engage them in a discussion?' he asked …

My first suggestion was to get the old bastard to fall on his sword, especially as he'd failed to recognise that he was both the main problem and Superman. I, however, knew that this observation would not be taken kindly (other than referring to him as Superman, of course).

We worked together to change the format of the next six monthly meetings. Agendas were set, with objectives focused on idea generation, accountability and ownership.

As things started to become clearer, he agreed to form a team of Directors from his managers (although, these were only titles, not statutory positions). This approach gave his team some recognition of status, but only after the six month trial.

The announcement was well received by the team. I sat in the first meeting to facilitate only. Following this, I helped the MD pull ideas together (his way of saving costs ... tight fisted old git. Well, he is a friend, so I can say this!).

The MD was still left with the problem of participation and proactivity during the meeting.

When I facilitated, I handed each of them a set number of post-it notes. The MD got the same.

The first area of change discussed was around 'increasing sales and profit'.

Each of the managers (Director designates) were asked to use a post-it note for each of their suggestions. They had six notes in total and had to use them all. I was using some funky exercises to get them thinking without getting caught up in the zone of daily tasks, which turned out to be good ice breakers and helped focus the session.

At the end of this session, with ideas from the MD and eight department managers, we'd managed to generate 54 ideas.

At this point, we took a break. When everyone was back and settled, I presented their ideas, eliminating those that overlapped.

We discussed the net 28 ideas. Each of these were discussed and individuals clarified what they meant with their idea. Everyone had one voice, no one was shot down and, for the first time, they were treated like Directors. Everyone had free time to explain their suggestions, which I'd fixed onto the flip chart as a reminder. This also served the purpose of stopping them climbing down in the presence of the owner.

The session was important in that it allowed their voices to be heard. It was encouraging and it reinforced the fact that they were not alone in their thinking, as some of the ideas were shared.

Their ideas were then prioritised and championed by them, which required them to work together across functions to achieve their goals. This formed the basis of future updates with a report on progress on their initiative.

The 28 ideas in this instance were prioritised into 11 active projects owned by the Leadership Team. Each one had a series of tasks allocated, which were designed to take them from A to B. A strategy had been formed, or part of it, at least.

In the months that followed, it did go off the rails at times, proving that such things were best aided with the help of an independent chairperson, or facilitator. Eventually, we prioritised five main areas (including sales and profit as one of them), each with a set of priority projects with underlying actions agreed by the team.

The remaining projects were not discounted. They remained on the list as pending, and would form future 'next' projects after the priorities were dealt with.

Management meetings did change. They are still productive and based on open dialogue and shared accountability. The MD, still as tight fisted as ever, did promote his team to Directors as promised. He did tell me that he only speaks for himself now, the same as everyone else. Regardless of whether I believe him, he has made giant leaps forward to engaging and creating a team with ideas and future suggestions.

Try hard to give everyone the chance to be heard and have an equal voice to your own, they will pleasantly surprise you.

IT'S BEHIND YOU

A Leadership role is riddled with various issues, particularly when you are engaged with your teams. Just like a dead mouse on your doorstep from your cat.

It is great that they feel comfortable bringing these things to you (the staff that is, not the cat) as this keeps the flow of engagement smooth. It also helps staff solve problems more efficiently, and encourages their development via Leadership participation. Although, being too close to the problem can be problematic.

People talk about objective decision-making and coaching to teams. If you are immersed in the problem from the start, it is often difficult to remain objective, especially when the problem area is something you could resolve yourself. For instance, if there's a problem related to something you fixed in a previous role.

Another example where it would be challenging to remain objective could be in the case of a purchasing issue arising, where the supplier is a friend of the Leader.

The same applies to our teams. Let's be honest, we employ specialist people for their immersed expertise in each function, so objectivity irregularities will occur, and frequently … something we should be prepared for.

I have found reliance on non-executive advisers to be particularly good, especially when they have no responsibility to the Shareholders. They are merely brought in to help the Leader remain objective, and are an excellent use of budget.

Where non-executive advisers cannot be easily appointed, found or afforded, there is always another option, one that can be used in parallel or in isolation: your friends or your network. And I am not referring to the person you shared a room with at University, the one that went off surfing in some far-flung beach in Australia. I'm referring to the people you meet in everyday life, other Leaders. It's amazing just how supportive other Leaders can be of each other (assuming there is no competitive threat of course, or all bets are off). The Leader's role can be a lonely one, so it is useful to have other Leaders on board.

Given all Leaders gladly talk about their successes and how they got there, challenges will be shared and each can learn from the other. A slight ego often goes with the territory, and I can admit to this from my perspective.

When I worked with other Leaders, it was fantastic. It helped me crystallise the issue through objective eyes at times. Phoning a friend every time I hit a problem to solve would be a little pathetic. It would also make me question why on earth I got the gig in the first place. But, when meeting up at an event or a get together, where you can chew things over with them, you'll find that there's a chance they faced similar challenges. They will definitely have an opinion, that's for sure.

I also like to think that, in some small way over the years, I have helped them too (probably on how not to do it).

As such, the non-exec role does not need to be a formal appointment. If a formal appointment is possible, do it. It's an opportunity to set something up with someone who can ask the challenging questions, someone detached from your everyday world.

Okay, most of you have probably pictured a small green chap from 'Star Wars', a wizened old gent, the oracle, the source of Leadership knowledge and the guru of all things marvellous. Sorry guys, they do not exist in real life (although, by the time I turn 90, I could buy a cape and green face paint. I would make it through a fancy-dress competition).

On a more serious note, though, you need to consider someone you can lean on. Someone who does not threaten or will not fight your battles. They need to be able to talk to you directly without the fear of being shouted at in return. If the occasion warrants, they may call you an idiot and make you find your own answers via their challenging questions.

With this in mind, I formed my own Leadership style. If I needed this, then so did my teams. This is what they needed me to be for them, someone objective, somewhat detached from the detail but sufficiently focused and knowledgeable.

My 1-2-1 meetings with my team have continued in this way for many years. This style has allowed them the space they need to run their own functions without strong interference (unless required of course). It also allows them to open up to me without fear of recourse. In other words, we get there together with me playing my part, not interfering constantly, but filling an essential role.

This style evolved over the years, openness became a two-way street, and I shared my wider challenges. The outcome has been great. By sharing my challenges, they help me in my role, but it also enables them to learn and grow themselves. We help each other.

This is how I form Leadership Teams with the people who want to take up the responsibility, based on mutual trust and a passion for making a difference. I will talk more about this in another section.

My message to you now is about having the ability to see things beyond what is directly in front of you, which sounds easy.

In my early days, I used to work in a very fancy laboratory for a paint manufacturer, as a Chemist. My job was to research new non-toxic chemical additives for vehicle refinish paint systems. Pioneering stuff, indeed. We made small batches of the paint (clear coat lacquer) and sprayed it onto small panels before testing them via a multitude of systems and processes, then analysed the results. This is a prime example of where new thinking was applied to an existing product, a product that was manufactured on site and despatched to car manufacturers across the world on a 'just in time for delivery' basis.

As part of the quality checking process, before a batch left the factory, it was checked by the QA laboratory (they were not as high profile as my research lab, with just a few people working in squalid conditions in the manufacturing facility; a couple of old men cruising to retirement). They were responsible for making up the paint, spraying it onto a panel, then baking it before checking its appearance. Everything else had been tried and tested. Ah, so these guys were checking for contaminations only … easy then.

I was busy as usual in my high-tech laboratory, writing up my analysis of the latest change ingredient, when the boss popped in to see me. I was told that the Quality Assurance team were unwell and that Manufacturing needed someone to carry out QA checks on the batch of clear coat leaving at 2 p.m. to a car manufacturer (a big one) in the Northwest. I was chosen, handpicked to save the day (well, I was told to do it, or else ... but let me have my moment please!).

The sample was with me within seconds it seemed. The onsite chap from Manufacturing, who'd brought it over, was standing in front of me, anxious for my attention, whilst gazing in amazement at the glamorous facilities before his eyes. It was rare for non-research staff to gain access to brand new research facilities. It was all very high-tech, with high security as we also did work for the MoD. With the custom straightening of my tie, I calmly took the sample from him, like this was something of regular occurrence, something insignificant. In doing so, I made him even more anxious. Anyway, I told him I would have the result in the next 90 minutes.

Now, 'just in time deliveries' means just that. The paint batch arrives just in time to continue production. Car manufacturers carry little or no raw materials, reducing any chances of contamination, or shelf life issues, etc., but it did mean that there was little margin for error. Having said this, the same product was made every few days in the same place, by the same people, following the same formula. Realistically, then, there was very little that could, or ever did, go wrong, until today.

I prepared the small sample, sprayed it onto the 6 x 4 inch panel (the size of a photo) in my laboratory, which had a water fed extraction. To most of us, this means there was a waterfall going down the wall, which took overspray/ chemicals into it, drawing air down from in front of the person spraying, and therefore reducing contaminants in the air (I told you that it was high-tech – well, yes, in the late 80s, but please pay attention).

On the panel were spots, big spots, where the clear coat could not adhere to the surface. The sort of effect you get when you wax your car and it rains; the waxed surface doesn't get wet. Oh shit!

I had discovered acne of the paint; this was not good.

The tanker had already set off from the West of London to Northwest England. I realised that my day was about to get stormy. I sprayed another, same thing.

There was only one thing to do: PANIC like hell. I called the boss, who called Manufacturing. Within minutes a delegation of senior staff, most of whom I did not know, were crawling all over the place, asking questions as though they were all about to be fired. Well, at least, they were taking responsibility, I thought. And quite rightly!

An hour had passed and an executive decision had yet to be made. The problem had escalated to the Chief Chemist (the Technical Director, the Polymer Scientist of the Group, God 2) who reported to the CEO.

My attendance was requested. I waded through the thick, pile carpet of his wood-cladded office on the fifth floor (well, it was the 80s), accompanied by the others. Action taken based on the information being fed to the main man.

1. Order the tankers return immediately. Dispose of product. Thoroughly cleanse entire vehicle and report issue to the logistics Company for compensation claim
2. Commence manufacture of new batch of clear coat immediately. Have staff on overtime tonight at different facility – contaminated facility to be cleansed
3. Test contaminated sample in another lab, with another chemist – try to remove variables

Decisive Leadership at its best. His was the job I wanted there and then!

He told us that we had a serious silicone contamination. Heads lowered. I did not know what this meant, but it seemed that Silicone (used in all sort of things, including grease on valves) would have caused the effect seen. It was hard to get rid of. The blame was moved to the manufacturing and engineering teams.

I returned to my plush surroundings, feeling rather concerned but ultimately pleased with myself. Instead of imagining a car production line that was producing defective goods at an enormous rate, I basked in being the saviour of the day. Had I not been at work today, establishing the problem would have been a much larger task. I was a hero.

Two hours later, a second meeting was called, with the same attendees. This time, the Director did seem concerned and was more intrigued.

It seemed that the sample had been re-checked at another laboratory, by someone else. The results were fine. All attention turned to me.

I was asked if I used hair gel (well, it was the 80s). Oh dear. Yes, I did. Hair gel in those days contained silicone. Apparently, particles from it had been blown from my hair and onto the panel.

Strangely, he then smiled at me. 'I knew it,' he said, and with that, all action points were reversed. The tanker turned back towards the north, and there was no more panic. There was still the matter of the tanker being delayed and production halted for one hour or so. Ah well, so only 30 cars or so were not produced (you should have seen the faces of the others, though).

The Director had taken an action point to note all the common things that contained Silicone. He had taken time to look at things objectively, instead of worrying about the law suit the Legal Director was facing, the extra work created for the Manufacturing Director or the negative client publicity facing the Sales Director.

He was quick to pick up on myself being the only variable, where others had not. An objective view.

Had he not have found this, production would have stopped for half a day, with far more destructive implications (they were bad enough as they were).

He also recommended a different hair product for me, which I was thankful for. I still remember his smile when everyone else was angry. I assume it was because he had found the cause and it was not destructive in the long run. He recognised it was an easy correction, when others around him were losing their cool, finding it difficult to see beyond their own agendas.

Sometimes the problem is not in front of you but somewhere you least expect it. Take time to widen your perspective and recognise variables before making decisions.

STRESS AND THE CHEESE SANDWICH

At the point when I had become an MD myself, another successful MD and friend, told me that the role of Leader was a lonely existence.

Think of a piece of rather expensive, and exclusive, cheese in a sandwich. Picture your favourite bread, covered in pickle, that's the image I leave with you.

The two slices of bread represent the Shareholders and your team. The Shareholder slice keeps you in situ, they invested in you and pay rewards to you, which can be lucrative.

The other slice, your team, cossets you with their support, their attention and helps you maximise all the results you collectively achieve.

The pickle represents, of course, the problems, challenges and daily crap that hits you from all directions.

Naturally, you are the cheese: revered by some and acknowledged by most as the most expensive single ingredient, someone who adds flavour to the main event.

Or, you could see it another way:

As an essential ingredient that, at times, fails to add the flavour required. But it is a necessary flavour required to counter the excessive pickle. There are far too many problems that influence the flavour you bring.

The bread slices compress this set of challenges from both sides, squeezing you, holding you in and restricting the parameters within which you move.

Crikey, who's leading who here? And so, you end up being a servant to everyone's happiness, making you popular with their pals, and you allow their flavour to dictate the taste of the business.

You could just throw away the pickle. Although, I can assure you these are not the sort of problems that just go away.

Ultimately, a great sandwich maker (and I make a pretty good ham cheese and pickle myself, I can tell you), will know that a great sandwich allows the ingredients to work together. They also ensure it does not fall apart while keeping together the super ingredients, flavours which complement each other.

Okay, so all this talk of sandwiches has made you feel hungry ... See you after lunch ...

Welcome back.

So, an autocratic Leader or maybe a Leader who is a patsy to everyone's needs, represent the extremes. My preference is to be a Leader who can make all the flavours and ingredients work together.

This suggests the need for you to surround yourself with complementary skills. This set of freestanding skills can work every function well enough, without you, without failure. It should also work with the other teams and limit negative impact from one to another.

This gives the Leader the freedom to influence each team and each function. In doing so, the Leader can focus on the 'next' direction while these functions deliver the 'now'.

Though, it's quite common for things to go wrong. Many years ago, a person conducting a Psychometric test told me that, under stress, people revert to their true self, a level where you are ultimately comfortable and in control. This also happens with Leaders. The Psychometric test looks at how well balanced we are and which part of our profile extends under stress. It is an accurate prediction on how our behaviours will change. As humans, we are all susceptible to this, however balanced we believe we are.

So, it's possible for a Leader to tread on the toes of one of the other Directors when stressed, particularly if this was a function the Leader had previous experience in.

Therefore, it stands to reason that, the more experienced you are as a Leader, the greater chance you have of distancing yourself from each individual function. Thereby maintaining balance even when under pressure. Conversely, a Leader emerging from, say, a Sales Director position could easily revert to playing the role of the Sales Director.

When this happens, and it does (I experienced this myself. Sadly, it also happened to people I reported into), the balance of skills changes, the flavour is altered and the overall taste is often ruined.

Sometimes, the Leader with the balanced skill set must jump in to help or to fix a specific problem. This is an unavoidable part of the role but, unfortunately, it can be great fun, particularly when results are poor. By demonstrating to Shareholders that you are adding immediate, visible value, your results profile is enhanced.

When this happens and continues over a long period, retaining control of the situation as a Leader becomes much harder as, up to this point, you were working as a peer with your team. As this status lingers, the team starts to see you siding with your chosen favourite function, your true flavour, rather than being the balanced, objective person they once looked up to.

Meanwhile, other Directors start to form strong cliques, primarily against you, to oppose your support with your favourite function. Well, why not? They also need to restore the balance of flavour. In essence, they are doing your job.

Ouch, serious stuff. Yes, indeed.

I once had to dismiss a Sales Director, due to an unfortunate act of gross misconduct.

Given his salary, the costs of re-hiring and the recruitment fee (you know where this is going), the Shareholders collectively suggested that I fulfilled this role. They knew that I had been a Sales Director (many years before). They wanted me to lead the client facing and marketing teams myself. It was, after all, something I could do, and the savings would be appreciated by the Shareholders.

This was my stress point, the point where my behaviour could change, and it hit me, like an unexpected sting from a jellyfish while taking a gentle swim in the sea. What was I to do?

I had certainly not expected this. Calmly, I was moving to replacing him, despite the candidates lined up. My Shareholders were almost complimenting me on my ability to take on this role (a rare event indeed). I was being flattered by them. I needed to consider this.

Yes, I thought, I can do this. I can make a fine go of it, too. I began thinking like a Sales Director and all the things I could do as MD: running the sales function, the abuse of power, the influence I would bring; we would be an unstoppable force ... woah! Hold on my friend. Danger, danger!

What the hell was going on?

Yes, I was flattered by the fact the Shareholders believed I could run the sales and marketing team. But I needed to stop and remind myself as to why I was here. I was being paid to do another job, based on the skills I brought to the whole Company and the achievements we had made to date. My Leadership style, balanced views, collaborative and democratic system was why I was here, and it was working well. I was a sandwich with all the right flavours, ingredients and support, but I was being squeezed, and about to be saturated by pickle, a flavour that would taint me. I recognised it would be difficult to shift this and it would affect my ability to restore balance. I was on a slippery slope.

I pushed back. The Shareholders had a look on their faces, something akin to feeding them vinegar. As if to say, 'How dare you oppose our decision?'

I reminded them of why they needed a Leader, and what a Leader does. I reinforced that the replacement Sales Director was essential in maintaining balance, leaving me to be the objective Leader.

The vinegar faces remained in situ. Well, it was a look I was familiar with. So, rather than please them, I remained steadfast in my view, something I have never regretted.

I constantly remind myself just how close I had come to falling into the trap. I didn't see it coming. That was the most shocking part. Despite a wealth of experience of dealing with this, on numerous occasions, it will always be a constant battle.

Reminding yourself of why you are a special ingredient is something that needs repetition. Otherwise, a stressful event will force you towards something you are capable of, but should not be doing for too long.

I often read my Psychometric profile (I am a bit sad like that) and remind myself of the fact that I need people around me, people who have specific functional desires and experiences. These are my complementary flavours, the ones I need to succeed.

The Leader is not the most important person; the success of a Company is the sum of all its parts. An objective Leader forms part of this and is an essential, something that must never be forgotten.

THE DESIRABLE ONES?

Earlier, I touched upon the sale of a Company I was managing. During the due diligence process, where the buyer conducts a full in-depth audit of every process, every person, every invoice and every document to get an idea of the full package, I was asked to list my top 10 most important employees. The buyer was a large American Finance Corporation that hoped to acquire 100% of shares and integrate us into their UK subsidiary. Sensible stuff, of course.

How do you filter out these people when you run a service business that carries no fat or excess? I knew one thing for certain … I would not be one of those in the top 10 if I had to choose.

Cheekily, I did provide a list, which was rejected as it consisted of all employees, except myself. I had not intended to inflame our buyer. I merely made the point that all staff play their part. Why do we need them otherwise?

We had generated profits in the upper quartile of our industry for the past two years. It was clear our headcount was necessary, both for the delivery of the 'now', and to achieve our 'next' growth.

Over the days that followed, the conversations became increasingly fractious: why was I deliberately avoiding this vital question?

If you look carefully at any process, manufacturing or otherwise, it is obvious that it is made up of its component parts. No one part of the process can survive without the interaction of the other.

I can also simplify and illustrate this by taking a watch apart (not one of those modern things, but a watch with perpetual movement, winding mechanism, etc.). When you look inside, you will marvel at its craftsmanship, and the intricacies of the movements of the many parts. There's probably a hundred or so individual pieces. Now ask yourself, 'Which of these parts are the most important 10 pieces?'

So, you sit there with your magnifying glass (as any buyer would do with our due diligence documents), looking, analysing and wondering which pieces one could do without. In the curious intricacy behind the watch's movement, I have no doubt that, if you took one piece out, something could go wrong. The watch could even cease to function at all. Why else would a Swiss watch maker put all these fiddly bits in there?

The watch components aren't there to add weight, increase cost or for the sake of unnecessary complexity, none of which adds value or function.

If we think of the watch as a Company, there is (in my strange mind) a direct comparison.

The Company exists as a working machine. It is only effective, reliable and valuable when each piece works well, performs its task and allows others to do theirs unimpeded.

In a people business, this is a true representation.

If one person is removed, leaves, or is not functioning at the right pace or effectiveness, others are strongly impacted, and could even fail to perform.

The role of the Leader is to ensure this does not happen or, when it does (and sadly it does), they get things moving and back on track.

This is true of the autocratic Leader. If the Leader acts as a bottleneck to decisions, through stalling decisions, inertia and other delays, other functions will reflect this pace, creating a knock-on effect on everyone else. In short, the watch stops and starts. Its natural flow is interrupted. This is not an extreme example, it is reflective of real life. The ineffective Leader, being the all controlling, all important person, can bring the process of decision-making (and therefore the business) to a halt. Perhaps this is a little dramatic, but they can certainly hinder it from moving at the pace it is rightly capable of.

So why did he ask me to list the 10 most important people?

I recognise that in any Company acquisition, we look at efficiency through identifying duplication and eliminating it, for example. How was I supposed to respond, though? I was unaware of the process the buyer was following; an impossible insight for me to gain, of course.

The new Group MD asked that I refine the criteria for this list further. The criteria, at that point, focused on performance, with the intention of removing those performing poorly.

Flippant as ever, I confirmed that any poor performance issues had been addressed, through coaching and support, or the poor performers had already left. What were they trying to achieve?

Eventually, we settled on the restricting the list to being the 'Top Team' and the 'Managers'. This was enough to reflect the many processes that maintained the effective flow of work and information. The lists totalled 20 people, but a compromise had been made based on seniority rather than my opinions. They were still up against a stained backdrop of a firing range that existed to satisfy only their long-term curiosity of possibilities. It solved no major purpose (in my opinion).

The Top Team was an important factor in maintaining a long-term grip on the managerial processes.

Similarly, in my Software days (as well as in other industries), our managers and Leadership

Teams were formed through an election process (over a course of time), aimed at keeping people on the board based on their contributions. If other board members felt that their presence was indeed valuable, supportive and essential to the Company and their own roles – we had the essential parts to create a working machine.

Perhaps controversial to some, but I did this (in numerous industries) by asking each member of the board to vote for a person, other than themselves, to receive a bonus based on the value of their overall contribution over the course of a month, and at the board meeting.

The people with the highest votes received a payment, a reward, but the board's opinions were the most important aspect. Over the course of time, it was expected that the board would reduce in size. In real terms, though, there was a rather obvious gap after just a few months. Presence on the board was clearly justified by the collective views of the rest of the group.

Despite sounding a little harsh, it worked. The objective was to get the team to take accountability, and not rely on myself, as Leader, to decide the operations board structure that would concentrate on local process management. It was a significant step in creating next generation Leaders and a step towards process owner accountability.

I have met MD's and CEO's, who, by their own admission and conversely to my views, think they are the most important part of their Company. Using the head and body analogy: you know, chop off the head and the body dies.

I was saddened for them. They resided in their self-important bubble, which I could only expect to burst one day, when they least expected it.

I would also be concerned for the teams they managed. I hoped these self-important people would not create bottlenecks and inertia via autocratic decision-making.

LET'S PUT FRED
ON A COURSE

Training is an essential part of our professional learning, and, at times, we all need this.

Although, I often wonder whether sending senior team members on a training course is somewhat of a cop-out for Directors. Does it help Directors shift the blame or problem on to someone, or somewhere else, in the hopes it will be dealt with?

Not all senior staff appreciate going on a course. I have felt like this, too.

'Hello Fred. We have arranged for you to attend a training course, at considerable expense, but it is a great investment in your future.' Gee thanks, boss.

If I were Fred, though, I'd feel lost. What was being said about me? Was I failing somewhere, somehow? I obviously need help, and my results may need to improve. Although, I have had good feedback from my Group CEO. So what prompted them to send me on further training?

Yes, this was definitely a message: pull your socks up, man, or else. Fred's left thinking, I do not want to attend and I doubt I will learn much. Yet, if I refuse to go, my career will probably be dented. It could also send a message of disrespect to the Company.

So, what exactly am I lacking? Ah okay. The course itself offers some clues: soft skills, and management. Hang on, I am a great coach to my team. I look after 60% of the group Company's staff. Shit, that's a kick in the teeth.

I view my boss with suspicion now. We were so open with each other. How could his attitude towards me have changed? Perhaps he couldn't find the means to inform me that I was failing. Instead, he put some distance between us. This was a bad day. I loved my job. I was good at it, at least that's what I was told. Hell, yeah, I know I am doing well. The results say it all. Look at the feedback on Best Companies, they think I am a great Director.

I met with the boss and skirted around the awkward subject, like a flame dancing around a fire, blowing in the night wind. Tell him, tell him.

So, I told him. The confrontation felt good to me. I was in the driving seat and let him have it.

He seemed devastated, like someone just threw away his winning lottery ticket. His right-hand man was being so negative. This was not right. This was not the man he had employed, given share options to. Why was the Director so de-motivated? The sudden shock my boss encountered would have been equivalent to me resigning, sticking two fingers in the air at him in some form of rebellious assault.

We cleared the air, thankfully, and resolved our issues.

His training investment in me followed previous attempts of offering training to suit my needs, based on my perspective. I had failed to recognise that I needed help or support and had always turned previous offers of training down. I was a one man show, master of my own destiny, I was doing well. Why would I need training?

So, although this was a genuine attempt at investing in me, I had not been able to self-criticise and identify where I could use some help. Having said that, in all honestly, the things I needed were not something I felt could be covered in a course. I was not attempting to belittle the training course model at all.

I highlighted that, rather than send my direct team on a course, I typically spent some time coaching them on soft skills that could add real life experiences to their existing great talent.

My time was given freely, regularly and specifically focused on the challenge of the day or month. The praise I received was reward enough for my time invested in them.

That's it! What I really needed was time with my boss. The training he was offering would only enhance my skills. Although the objective was valid, the message I received was taken out of context, by myself. My interpretation suggested I was failing, rather than seeing it as a means of becoming a great Leader like him.

Subsequently, we set up regular 1-2-1 meetings, rather than just meet at the monthly board meetings. The 1-2-1 ensured we talked openly about everything, where there were no negative implications of me acknowledging my failures, my concerns and my challenges. Similarly, we discussed my ideas, and he imparted his views and suggestions, based on his own experiences.

He was now coaching me and, guess what? I was learning at an unexpected pace. Wow.

Knowledge was flowing into me like a scene from the film 'The Matrix'. I was like Keanu Reeves, but without the looks, fame and wealth (but, hey, I can dream).

I soon recognised that we all need help, despite doing well and staying on top of our game. There are many things that can happen, both unpredicted and unplanned for. Talking to others with different experiences and asking advice does not mean you are weak, that you do not have the answers. It helps put your ideas into perspective and offers different views, some that will challenge your thinking.

Since then, I countered my loneliness by talking to a network of other Leaders. Simply talking about very little and listening to them can be inspiring, engaging and hugely rewarding in so many ways.

Who do you talk to, or ask advice from?

Similarly, who in your team do you coach in the same way? I don't mean manage, but coaching them to build their skills and confidence for the next role.

This is where succession planning comes in.

Companies talk about this, but rarely does it happen. It's easy to identify someone with talent, someone who wants the next job; my nine-year-old can do that.

Succession planning is not just about saying that Fred can take over if I am moved to Hong Kong. It is about investment in a person or people that prepares them to take on the next challenge before the opportunity arises.

Many Leaders do not do this as they feel threatened by people who can do their job. They fear the person will leave or take over from them.

A very famous Leader once stated: you should train your staff well enough so that they can leave you; treat them well enough so that they do not want to. Great thought Leadership indeed.

Personal investment in people inherently comes with the risk that they will move on. Yet, this is not as common a problem when you treat them well, strengthen them for the future and continue to coach them to become the best version of themselves.

They do not forget your personal investment in them and it creates loyalty, especially when they feel well treated.

Your staff are always able to move on, and sometimes they will. Let me ask you, would you prefer to lose a team member, knowing you have helped them get there or would you rather lose them because you held them back? Either way, the outcome is the same. However, over the course of time your loyalty will see loyalty in return.

Regarding succession planning, do remember that it is pointless keeping this to yourself.

In my leasing days, I was offered a position outside the Company. I was doing well where I was getting noticed. I had achieved some status already. The new position offered a better status and more responsibility. Very flattering and maybe a jump too far at that stage. Yet, someone was showing interest. They were willing to invest in me and believed I could take on the role of Director Designate, with a view to becoming Director six months later.

I resigned in an instant, having accepted the position already. The conversation with the MD that followed confused me.

He seemed disappointed (hard to be sympathetic when I was on cloud nine, personally), and told me of the future plans they had in mind for me. Plans that had been in discussion for months by the board. In six months, they had expected these plans to materialise. My euphoria turned to confusion as I wrestled with this alternative. Moments seemed like hours as my face turned from smiles to a more serious me. I had felt great. But this confusion was now stressing me. What was I to do?

Regardless of the choice I made, I'd end up in the same position, within a similar timeframe. My current employer was familiar. I knew what I was doing, and knew that I had a great platform to launch from here. These people respected me … or did they?

Despite behaving like a Gemini at times, I am a true Sagittarian. Yet, an interesting dilemma does create confusion for the decisive-by-nature person.

I was facing a boss who had not engaged me, not talked to me about what I wanted and kept me at arm's length for ages. It was only when I resigned that he thought it necessary to outline this plan, a succession plan for me to progress. Was this genuine? Was I being managed?

I reflected on this for a few minutes, the opportunity sounded good. I then imagined how this would seem through the eyes of the new Company. They had taken the time to talk to me, find out what I wanted, had recognised my strengths and many development areas, and offered to help me fill the gaps. They did this without me asking. They did this at their own risk, not because of my decision-creating risk.

I did leave in the end. There is an important lesson to learn from this. It is not just to share your plans, which are essential, but to treat your team like they are new. Recognise that they have desires and ambitions. If I could treat my team like every moment of every day was an interview, what could I achieve?

A hell of a lot, that's what.

I talk about more about 'staff engagement' in other sections, but I hope you can see my logic?

The objective behind interviewing is primarily to find the perfect fit to your well-written job description. As I mentioned earlier, this rarely happens. Instead, we compromise on the candidate.

What if we made the job fit the candidate … a romantic notion, I hear you say, and highly impractical. Well, yes, perhaps it is for a new hire coming into an existing rigid structure. If the structure was more flexible, where team members did more of the things they excelled in and enjoyed … Wow, look at your productivity now, my friend!

If you know your staff, you will know what they desire, what excites them, which, in turn, will help you visualise their ideas in practical terms and guide your development of them.

This is a basic human trait. We all have things we are good at. The role of the Leader is to get the best from each team or person.

So, rather than wait until they're ready to leave you, work with them at creating a role with responsibilities moulded to them, allowing them focus on doing one thing well.

In all the jobs I had, there were 20-40% of tasks I did not enjoy. Is this just me? No, we are all human, and whilst variation can be stimulating, you will note that people will have similar issues.

So, if five people perform a similar role, we will have 5 x 20% (say) of their time where they are not enjoying their task.

Why not get them enjoying their role 100% of the time through giving them the tasks they like and excel at. Eliminate the 20% of wasted time? But, who picks up the slack? Easy, someone who loves doing just that 100% of their time.

Five people (ineffective 20% of their time) then become five effective people, doing what they enjoy. Logically, this works, so why are we constrained to the job description?

What are you waiting for? Change the job description!

I recall doing this in my recruitment days.

We had a network of small branch offices located across England, each with a team of four.

In each branch, the team were expected to (as a basic minimum guide):

- Be good, driven sales people
- Be great at finding candidates

- Be good at administration, payroll, statutory checks, etc.

This is typically how recruitment companies worked back then and, sadly, many still do. To find such diverse talents in a person may sound difficult.

Finding someone to do this was easy as the recruitment world is full of recruiters in every town. An offer of an additional £1k per annum, and people would move.

The Company was losing money, and like other recruiters, we had a 70% turnover of staff. It is a problem that still exists (although, hopefully, the rate has declined a little since?).

I hope you recognise just how much of a problem a 70% turnover creates. To retain staff, we engaged them through discussing their likes and dislikes.

We typically had three groups at minimum. Yep, you guessed it: sales people, recruiters and administrators (who knew, eh?).

Putting these people into revised roles worked, although, sadly no one wanted to do the admin. Well, that was an easy role to fill, find someone who does like admin.

So, after a few role changes, redundancies and hiring new administrators, we fixed an age-old issue.

The staff were motivated: some were motivated by money, those who loved finding people jobs were justly rewarded and administrators did their role accurately and diligently.

At some point though, administration was centralised further. Despite this, the same principle continued – the focus on doing one thing well.

Our job as Leaders is to have the confidence to lead an organisation transformation in an industry that still follows conventional means. Tradition dictates that we work this way.

Break with tradition and be bold.

Our staff retention was higher as they were listened to. They did the job they wanted and numerous barriers were removed from their path to success. Their managers could measure their achievements and progress, unable to hide behind other things, bringing focus and enjoyment.

After all, a happy person will perform better than one who comes to work de-motivated, even if it's just 20% of the time.

The same process is true for managers and Leaders. If some of the tasks a Leader must do are a burden, a curse or indeed difficult, chances are, there will be another member of the team willing to help ease this burden, whilst developing their skills for the future.

WISDOM FOR THE OLD AND ENERGY FOR THE YOUNG?

There was a time in my outsourcing days when I wanted to hire a recruit for a client division.

As a Director, I knew what I wanted, someone energetic, someone who would inspire their team and work passionately in helping to drive results.

As was usual for this large Company, HR got involved in the interview process, the creation of the documents and the running of the selection criteria, profiling, etc., which was very beneficial.

In doing so, the candidate who shone above all was a woman aged 63. I knew of her work, and I was really impressed.

The Company CEO was in that day and asked what I was doing. Naturally, we had a productive discussion, although his final comments were really disturbing.

He challenged my decision to potentially hire her. He implied that we were a young, dynamic Company, and that we should be hiring young people.

Apart from the discriminatory angle of his comments, which offended me, I was shocked to think that this person was being discounted (by him, not me), based on age, written off for retirement with no future career prospects.

This owner was much younger than myself, but that does not excuse his behaviour. He was known for being a great entrepreneur (and was hugely successful). Yet, I felt he was not a good people Leader.

As our discussion progressed, he insisted we did not hire her.

This candidate was more energised to work than people half her age. She had the experience to challenge me, which was what we needed, and the maturity to work with teams and clients. Yet, her age was considered a show stopper?

I have intervened in the hiring process where older candidates have applied and been rejected by my team. Probably for the same reasons.

It is true that some people over a certain age want to take a more relaxed view on life, but this does not apply to all.

People I have met, interviewed or even hired in their sixties have demonstrated a genuine desire to work. They bring with them a huge amount of experience, and often exhibit a loyalty way beyond that of a fresh college graduate.

Their experience also adds an appreciation for a Company with a great culture. It may be that they were not treated well sometime along their career (not just because of age one might hope), possibly due to the general disregard for people that some Companies have.

I do not advocate an entire workforce of people aged fifty-five and over, either. There needs to be a mixture of people, based on the skills and experiences they can bring.

In my Software days, I was quite proud of the diverse culture we had. There were 14 different nationalities in our team.

Just as young and old help create a diverse mix, so too will a mixture of other cultures, religions and sexes.

Some Companies do not see diversity as it was meant to be. For instance, some companies monitor it to tick the corporate responsibility box, just to demonstrate that they are being an equal opportunities employer.

Okay, monitoring it and shouting about is not necessarily a bad thing. There is a chance it will attract others to come forward, so there is a positive side to it.

But doing this for the wrong reasons is not a great idea. It should be done to ensure there are benefits all around, through a mix of better skills, different ideas and global reach.

I do still wonder whether organisations attract diverse workforces for the right reasons, though.

I would sooner sponsor (at a cost) a worker from India to work in the UK if their skills are what I need. I would not hire them to prove to someone that I appoint from different ethnic groups.

So, I am rattling on about diversity, and trying desperately to avoid a political argument around immigration as I do not like tomatoes being thrown at my head (or any other part of me for that matter).

Diversity, though, can be closer to home than we may think, even among a bunch of 40-year-old white men, for example.

Once, when I was working for a large recruitment Company, I attended a Cultural awareness programme (well, we were spread across 47 countries, so it was a good investment).

The programme took place in some glamorous castle setting in Switzerland, the former home of the major Shareholder (one of his many spare properties).

The training programme consisted of two sessions, each one week in duration. We were there to learn, yet the programme seemed a little lighter than most courses in the first few days. There was plenty of time to relax, socialise and have fun in the underground complex where there was a swimming pool, a beer cellar, hot tub, plunge pool and steam room.

Did I mention the bowling alley? Well, this place had one. It was all fantastic, especially when coupled with as much Swiss chocolate as you could manage (and I could manage some, I tell you).

To start off, we were split into groups of eight (randomly, or so it seemed), each forming a work group, to debate a simple topic: 'The definitive colour of the sky and surroundings' … were they serious? I thought. I have been sent on a hippy holiday to get pissed, chill out and socialise with my colleagues from around the world. I wondered how much of a liar I would have to become when back in London, where I would have to tell them how tough this course was, whilst stuffing my face with chocolate.

As it turned out, the debate was rather difficult. When I say difficult, imagine friendly talks taking place between the Arabs and the Jews over a simple topic of ownership based in Jerusalem. Okay, hold that thought.

I honestly do not intend to spark a political debate. It's just a pertinent example for this case … we simply could not agree … we could not agree on the colour of the bloody sky for goodness sake.

We had to be definitive. There was no scope for wishy-washy answers and we only had two hours to come to an agreement.

I suddenly realised why the castle offered its delegates so much recreation space. As I glared into the Italian guy's eyes, I wondered why he could not accept my view: the sky was light blue with patches of grey and white, surely?

He insisted that the sky was grey, with patches of white and a little blue.

So, we all agreed on the range of colours, but we could not define it precisely enough.

How could our country presidents put us through this debacle? It was a complete waste of time, my valuable time. Did they not know how busy and stressful my job was? Did they even care?

I needed to relax, it was the best alternative to shooting someone (my counterpart from Poland), when the programme facilitator entered the room.

It was a battlefield, notwithstanding the fact we were alive (just). Everyone was battle worn, bruised and battered from the cuts and blows from our fellow Global Directors from other territories. The only thing we agreed on was that we wanted this painful ordeal to end so we could go back to our jobs, and that fact we all hated each other. I honestly think we hated each other at that point. Emotions were high, there was definitely no love here.

The poor facilitator seemed calm as he entered the room. Clearly, he is an idiot, I thought. How could he leave us for two hours, then turn up looking like a ray of sunshine? Naturally, we hated him too.

Thankfully, lunch was a finger buffet, else I would have used the cutlery as a weapon and attacked someone. Or I may have needed the cutlery to defend myself … hatred was flowing from all of us, proportionally.

We joined other groups while we ate, clinging in comfort to our fellow countrymen and women only. We discussed the farcical nature of this programme, the audacity, the humiliation, the idiots and … mmm, the finger buffet!

Looking around the room, it was obvious things were not good. Despite everyone having the same view, individuals in each group just could not get along. We were given a simple task that should have taken no more than five minutes.

After lunch, we were scheduled to attend the second session. For two hours, from 2 p.m. to 4 p.m. Oh no! That's it, I was calling my secretary for flights home.

The second session began with the programme Leader taking control. He explained that our next task was just for fun – we were going to repeat the morning session (is he for real? Now he had our collective hatred). He must have been unhinged, a masochist of giant proportions … more chocolate was needed.

Oh, but it wasn't exactly the same as in the morning. This time, the names were shuffled and we were placed in different groups. As we made our way towards our syndicate rooms, we passed members from our previous groups. A stream of scathing looks was enough. There was no need for words, interpretations or explanations.

And so the debate recommenced. This time, we were seemingly more engaged, more approachable. An hour later and we were all laughing. Surprisingly, there was a lot more agreement. Had someone cast a spell upon us, played a trick, or put something in the drinks? No, we were just people getting on together and working towards a common goal.

After the session, we retired to the beer cellar and all the other lovely facilities (the beer cellar, then) to relax. It was 4.30 p.m. We had time to read emails, make calls and chill out.

The next morning, we were told to go to the grand hall. It didn't look too grand with all its masking tape on the dark marble and wooden floors.

The tape had a purpose, though. It formed the outline for a large, nine-box grid, each with numbers inside and a piece of paper. We glanced at it with curiosity while the programme Leader (another ex-military officer) took charge.

He mentioned the 360 feedback they had gathered on us prior to being flown out to Switzerland, from our staff, ourselves, our country President and our peers.

The exercise was knitted together, by magic perhaps? Or, more likely, Psychometric profiling, and the results were shared with each of us in a printed, personalised pack.

Before we were given the chance to read these, we were given a number and asked to stand near the square on the floor grid that held the corresponding number.

After everyone had found their square, we realised we were back with the people from the first session. Although, we were all standing far enough apart, for obvious reasons.

We were then given another number, and moved accordingly. Strangely the second set of numbers placed us back with the people from the second session.

The programme Leader (the British delegates called him Colonel Mustard; the Latin American colleagues did not get the joke) addressed us once again.

He walked us through the structure of our printed packs. He emphasised that our profiling results would either conflict or complement each other, therefore reflecting groups one and two respectively.

The structure of the sessions had not been random, then. They had intentionally placed people with similar Psychometric profiles together in the first session. As we all had similar strengths in particular areas, it explained why we were not able to agree. We were much too alike.

We recognised that the second session consisted of people whose profiles complemented each other.

We were more helpful, and therefore able to get more from each other. It was a good lesson learnt: that each type of profile was necessary to bring a well-balanced and democratic system to life.

So, they were not idiots after all!

Since then, I have tried to embrace the magic of Psychometric profiling on teams. Not necessarily to decide who to hire, but to make sure we understand each other's strengths, appreciate each other's qualities and recognise why we behave differently.

Since this Swiss course, I have become better at surrounding myself with people who complement my own profile, and vice versa.

This is a great way of building teams, and it also gives the Leadership Team an appreciation of each other. Beyond team building, it also helps to ensure that progressive meetings take place with healthier debates, rather than arguments, provided everyone has one equal voice and their views are uninterrupted.

I have used many different Psychometric profiling methods over the years, and have always been led by those who understand how to use these properly.

The most important aspect of this is to bring teams together, have fun and a share experiences.

And so, 'diversity' is an essential part of life. If everyone was the same, there would be the odd breakout of mild professional violence, for good measure and little progress.

YOU ARE THE WEAKEST
LINK – GOODBYE

Some of you may have seen the quiz show. I have never been on it myself but, in this section, I will highlight the benefits of listening and taking an interest.

It's quite a common notion for Companies to have policies that require their staff to be at their desks from nine to five, when there isn't really a need to be physically present all that time.

In most of my roles as Director, we introduced flexible working practices, which were based on getting the job done, rather than the false sense of security inherent with nine to fives.

Whilst I recognise the need for discipline, rules and structure, sometimes we need to recognise that people's lives do not work around nine to five. In some organisations, we see people waiting for others to finish a task before they can do theirs. In this instance, it may be better for them to work after 5 p.m., once all the information is available. Thereby giving them time off during the day (provided the job gets done). This can be more productive, empowering and enjoyable for the team. I realise this is not practical in all roles, and this is where staff engagement comes in.

Let's take a case where a staff colleague has a family member in hospital 50 miles away. They leave the office, have a quick dinner at home, then visit the hospital, returning late. It's expected that, after three nights of this, they would be exhausted. Would their performance at work be affected? If you are engaging your teams sufficiently, you will be aware of the circumstances affecting them, both in and out of work.

A manager could suggest they visit the hospital during the earlier visiting hours, come home early, then work from home over dinner, if this suited them.

We referred to this in another section. My point here is relevant to the team being 'in the room'.

It is a false belief when one thinks that having staff physically present at their desks from nine to five results in eight hours (give or take breaks) of productivity. I would rather have my people working the way that gets results.

I remember a great manager who worked in my team in my recruitment days. He was really good with people and had outside of work interests (as most people do, of course) that kept him busy until late at night (no, he was not an alcoholic stalker!).

He knew he was never productive between nine and ten in the morning, so his hours were changed from ten to six. This small change gave him that much needed additional hour in bed, which meant that he was more productive over the same number of hours.

Similarly, I remember a time during my outsourcing days. I worked for a Company that was some three and a half hours away (yes, each way).

The owner had rescheduled a series of board meeting to take place every Friday at 4 p.m., followed by drinks, instead of on Mondays as usual. I was keen to attend, of course. Although, the things I'd be missing by not being at home until midnight on Friday did cross my mind. I left soon after this. Friday nights at home were rather precious to me, and they still are.

This reinforces what we talked about regarding listening. Listening to the views of others, learning more about them and understanding implications is key before action is taken. It should not stop you making the decision, though. Instead, it will give you valuable insight on the fallout or other implications of your actions following that decision.

I learned a valuable lesson from NOT listening once. My mind was a million miles away at the time of the incident, but I can now share it.

When my Company was acquired, I was expected to attend a meeting about long-term planning. The meeting had been planned to run over several days and no detailed explanation or direction was given in regard to what the meeting was about, other than the headline: strategy two days away. Really? Ouch.

I was not engaged in any way on this meeting. My doing, not the fault of the CEO, I add. All that was required of me was that I comply and attend, so I accepted.

Then fortune knocked on my door. A major client needed me to attend a series of important briefings. The dates coincided with the nights away. Clients must come first, surely. The Group CEO agreed, reluctantly, but it worked well.

As the client meeting only lasted a few hours on the first day of the 'big internal off site meeting', I arrived there in time for dinner (well, a man's got to eat!).

I turned up, not wanting to be there, rebellious to a fault and suitably unimpressed.

I woke up fresh and early the following day and missed the first day's sessions (I was sharp. Surely I could catch up).

We got into breakout groups to debate topics that would help the business grow. The Group CEO, had put some great things on the table. She was (and still is) an inspiring Leader. The topics she came up with stimulated our brains and helped us work better in teams. I was confident we would make great progress.

Then, playing the part of a concerned colleague (or assassin?), one of my fellow Directors (someone from the acquiring party), decided to help me understand the nature of the meetings.

The game was all about the player with the weakest link, just like the television programme, but with careers at stake, not some cheesy prize.

He revelled in the knowledge that my Company had just been acquired by the Group Company he had been familiar with for years. The newcomers, apparently, would be ganged up on and voted against.

He explained that, as a newcomer, I would not be wise to vote against any of the old guard, as they would vote against me. The one with the most votes would end up leaving the Company. These days thankfully, a more formal process is in place. Years ago, it was not as stringent so we were able to play 'The weakest Link', and I was to be the one chosen to leave.

As a newcomer, I was stuffed before I'd even started. Everyone else was just looking out for one another.

During the sessions that followed, my mind was pre-occupied. I wanted to be at home, not here wasting time waiting for the inevitable vote off, the public humiliation. I knew I would be embarrassed in front of 30 people. The aim was to reduce the Leadership Team headcount by one each month (so I was told. Others nodded in agreement when he told me, so it seemed credible).

The debates were good. I was with a good, strong successful team. Although, when the Group CEO entered the room, the dynamic changed. Suddenly, everyone was more concerned about impressing the boss, rather than just getting on with the task. What a shame. Perhaps the Group CEO was the Weakest Link. Yes, this was my way out. I had the chance to preserve myself and stop myself from being overtly attacked and humiliated this way. It was dangerous, but could buy me some time in the general company of others.

We all went back to share and discuss our ideas with the rest of the group.

Preoccupied as I was, I was not listening to the COO talking about the last two days. I was doodling, you know, with my pen creating wild circles on my paper, preparing myself for what was to come next.

The COO then interrupted my doodling to say, 'David, are you okay with this?'

What? I wasn't even listening, not at all. All eyes were upon me.

He went on: '… the Weakest Link. Are you okay? Do you understand the rules?' … 'Yes,' was the only response I could come up with. I stood up to deliver my well pondered political verdict, believing this was my cue to take the floor as the newcomer.

They all stared. I wondered whether I had something growing out of my head, judging by the stares I was getting. Some were open-mouthed.

Undeterred, I continued to the front of the room. The Group COO said nothing, neither did the CEO. I then realised that the COO was staring at me like everyone else in the room. Now I did have a complex. The room maintained its eerie silence.

I stood up straight and stated that the Weakest Link was the Group CEO. That somewhat deflated the energy in the breakout groups, and dented the flow of ideas as everyone was trying to impress the boss rather than be creative. There I said it: the Group CEO was the Weakest Link, hoping that my colleagues would not gang up on me.

An atmospheric disturbance erupted, as painful as a nuclear bomb being detonated. Although no words were spoken, something was wrong, very wrong indeed.

The whole room looked away from me in an instant, as if I was something to be ashamed of. Oh dear, what I had I done?

The Group CEO looked as though she'd passed a death sentence for some nasty criminal act I'd committed. The Group COO broke the silence. He said he'd thought that I'd understood the rules and that he himself was shocked by my comments.

The rules were, it transpired, for each of us to place our votes anonymously in the box on the way out.

His embarrassment turned into my humiliation. I had not listened, purely as I had not wanted to be there, 'in the room'.

I have remained on friendship terms with the CEO and COO. This was a strong lesson for me, one I will not let happen again. Needless to say, I lost respect for the assassins who'd set out to poison me.

In the blink of an eye, I went from a successful, productive person to someone who was not paying attention. Someone who listened to one side of the story, was blinded by self-preservation and not taking the necessary time to listen to the whole story.

This is why I say that you can only have productive people who are engaged, people who know what they are doing and why.

It is human nature to drift, wander and lose concentration. Our lives are full of distractions. Some of these will be more important to our staff than the immediate work-related task.

Talk to your teams, to find out if something is eating at them and try and understand it. Giving them time out is not wrong if they can make up the time and be 'in the room' when they need to be.

The nine to five culture is not necessarily the best way to get results from everyone.

Back in my Software days, one of the Shareholders who came for the monthly board meetings that started at 10 a.m., was always punctual and respectful. One day he turned up very early.

A minute later, one of the software developers arrived, greeted the Shareholder at the door, then proceeded to his desk.

The Shareholder demanded that I discipline this chap, for stealing (time), for arriving late.

I reminded him of the flexible working policy. The Shareholder took this to mean that ten minutes either side of nine to five was acceptable, anything else was taking liberty.

After reassuring him that this chap worked until very late each night and that we had agreed for him to start at 10 a.m., he calmed down. Although, it was clearly hard for him to accept as there were no managers checking to see if he was still working at ten in the evening.

A good point. This is where a little trust, flexibility and appreciation of people's strengths, rather than just focusing on the negatives, seems to play an important role in staff loyalty, retention and happiness.

JUST SAY 'NO'

In a corporate business, most Leaders have other Shareholders, investors or parent companies that have a vested interest in seeing the Company become successful.

This can equate to a tough existence for the Leader. As is expected, human nature almost ensures that they will have their own ideas, opinions and methods, which they will want to dictate to the Leader.

In my Software days, my predecessor had been deemed as a failure, a loss-maker. Apparently, they had dragged a good business deep down into the abyss.

My skills were called upon. A short while after I started, I discovered an additional problem, one that was not easy to resolve –

Shareholder intervention.

As the Company was in such distress at the time, I was given complete autonomy in turning it around (the problems were so severe, it was likely that we only had six months before going bust).

After a few months, I had stopped the rot, so we were in a stronger position already. Although the haemorrhage had stopped, we still needed to remove the nastiness. So, I came up with a fixed plan to make it healthy again.

By this point, I had a better understanding of why the Company had failed and why my predecessor had fallen. Interference was on the list, although poor Leadership did play a major role.

When things started to improve, it was almost like a once broken toy being given new batteries. Suddenly, they were interested again.

And everyone wanted some level of involvement. After all, everyone wants to be part of success, but far away from failure as possible. This I understood. They were not being vindictive, it was just human nature, really.

The pressure on me to act on their instructions was immense. At the end of the day, they owned the Company. They had a right to do things their way. But no, I would not be pressured. This was what happened (I think) to my predecessor. They must have been under pressure to act in a certain way, which, in turn, triggered the detachment from owning the broken process and re-attach once it was working once more.

The Shareholders found this easier to accept as things were working, so they kindly left me to it. Life is never straight forward, it is always full of ups and downs.

During the recovery process, we experienced a decline. Our largest client had used up all their budget, forcing them to stop spending for nine months (we did not know the exact timescale then). It was a devastating blow to an otherwise good, progressive performance.

Then came the visit. The delegation of the Shareholders turned up, unannounced. They were not at all friendly and were, understandably, concerned about their lifelong investment.

I was asked to make several redundancies, change what I was doing in favour of their suggestions and knee jerk into action. Again, these were all understandable reactions.

My instincts needed them to leave me to continue in my own way, as they had earlier. This time was different, though. Poor performance was upon me and my honeymoon period had ended.

Knowing myself, I was concerned that my pig-headedness would get in the way of my objectivity. At this stage, the easy option was to comply with their wishes. They would like me more for it and would probably be more supportive. However, this did not seem like the right way forward to me.

This is when the strength of the team came into its own. We collectively (once again) focused on the challenges and broke these down into bite-sized chunks. I then presented our plan to the Shareholders.

Whilst they were not pleased with my refusal to comply with their wishes, with threats of being sacked, they recognised that I was there to do a job and eventually gave me some more rope.

I followed my belief, and that of my team, and continued to act together with specific goals.

We stood together, not in blind, naïve friendship, but with adversity bonding us. We had agreed to a series of actions, and we stuck together.

As it turned out, our plan worked. It certainly was not easy, but consider the alternative?

Well, let's consider it shall we … it would have meant giving up, abandoning my cause, throwing away my own self-belief, belief in my team and the Company. What would that have made me? Not much really. Certainly not a Leader; not a man of strong beliefs. Equally, I would most certainly have dented my credibility with my team of Directors.

The role of the Leader, in this situation, was to inspire others and create and lead a modified vision based on new challenges, whilst remaining fixed on a belief in who we are and what we could achieve together.

Being able to see things that others cannot (because someone turns your lights out) is a skill. Not everyone has the ability to inspire others with their night vision. Nor is the ability to say NO in the face of extreme adversity. This is even harder when you are alone on a path that is criticised by those you rely on (for your income), but are still prepared to lead others along this path to eventual safety. I refer to this in other sections.

Many years ago, a client of mine complimented me on my ability to say NO to them when they started making demands on my Company, ones I did not support or agree with.

They were a large, American owned organisation, pushing for what they could get (and they were good at it). For us, this was a big National account, with its big brands. Who could refuse? (That would be me then, obviously).

I was not obnoxious. I was just prepared to go as far as I felt I should, based on my beliefs, which considered what we were doing for the cost of the service. I refused to budge beyond that.

We did get the contract. I remember the Purchasing Director and Treasurer asking me what training courses I had been on. They had spent a fortune on training their national sales team on negotiation techniques and nothing had changed (they said) with their diminishing sales margins.

Quite a compliment, but they had a point. Sales people represent the meat in the corporate negotiation sandwich of buyers and employers. They have to please both parties.

One party paying their wages, regardless of the margin they returned, the other offering them commission and success in the form of a sale. Which one would you be loyal to?

I have always spent time with the sales teams, helping them see things through the eyes of a Managing Director, in terms of what an MD looks for, and why we are how we are as Leaders.

This coaching time originated from something that happened many years ago. I met a Procurement Director in a very large, City-based firm. So impressed was I, that years later, when he set up on his own, I employed his skills to run a series of training sessions with sales people. This was in my outsourcing days.

We started off by making demands on them in a role play situation (based on a recent, real-life scenario they'd chosen, one where they had won a contract). This chap put his own objections into the scene and professionally made mincemeat of them. He took each one apart and ended up with reduced margins, lack of confidence and extra giveaways (this was an opportunity to remind myself that, at this stage, it was better to be in management than be a delegate).

We then allowed him to coach us through the concept of saying NO, with polite explanations and questioning to challenge the client, a concept quite alien to most sales teams at the best of times (and probably still is to some).

His insight and coaching was invaluable. Over the course of time, we saw improvements in the sales team's behaviour and reductions in giveaways.

Going back to my Software days, I recall a sales person asking me to support him with one of his new clients. They wanted us to commence work within a week, when our typical lead times were eight weeks. They also wanted a large discount, with free training thrown in.

This sales person was vastly experienced, so I respected his views. I wondered why they wanted this and asked him. His reaction seemed less than convincing. If we gave in, there would be a negative impact on our margins (financial; there was no room for error), and we would need to de-prioritise other clients who had commissioned our work before them. This was not good working practice, and certainly not something we liked to do.

I offered to call the client, which the sales person was not happy about. So, I invited him to join in on the call. I gave him the option of talking to them himself in case he felt I was going to ruin the deal. He declined the offer as he believed they would send me down the road with a flea in my ear, and I would back down.

As it happened, the client listened to my concerns. They understood the need for us to maintain our eight-week lead time, which in turn meant they could be reassured in the knowledge that they would not be let down by us gazumping them when another prospect came along. On the matter of discount, I explained that this was not a feasible way forward for us as we had just moved from loss to profit making. We wanted to be there for our customers in the years to come, unlike many of our competitors. They accepted 'NO' with reasoning and went ahead, contrary to the sales person's beliefs. The client had pushed for an early start as they were impatient, keen to move forward and, as they stated, 'if you don't ask, you don't get'. I think they also wanted to test our desperation. If we had given in, no doubt they would have made further demands down the line.

It is therefore more compelling to show staff what can be achieved, rather than just telling them. I will always say 'yes' when I can, but saying NO at the right time is still considered the best answer in certain cases.

What is the cost of saying YES, versus the risk of saying NO?

DEATH BY A THOUSAND CUTS

When it comes to making cuts, one does not necessarily mean staff cuts. Cuts can be in the form of positive negotiations with suppliers, reduction of waste (which is sensible regardless of how desperate one is), the consolidation of operations into one office or even ceasing corporate international travel for a few months.

Unfortunately, mention the word 'cut' and most will naturally worry about loss of jobs and insecurity. Before you know it, people are leaving in their masses, like rats escaping the corridors of the *Titanic* as it filled with cold, wet stuff.

When making changes or forming a plan to change something, it is important to consider the consequences of your actions, as there will, undoubtedly, be some.

People do not like change. These people often live in a state of insecurity, expecting change to be bad, continual and personal.

This mindset can be altered. If actions pertaining to change are thought through well enough, there will be good reason for you to consider making that change. Be open with your reasoning, you have nothing to lose. People need to be able to relate to the 'why' behind the change. They need to be able to knit together the backdrop for the actions in their own minds. Alongside this, for a change to materialise smoothly, people need to be able to determine the thought process as the human brain likes to be one step ahead, and forms its own projections and decisions as to whether logic has prevailed.

In doing so, a person's brain then seeks to apportion blame when change affects them. This often leads to the formation of negative projections on what is to come. We cannot eliminate this behaviour, but we can support them with the logic to make better, more informed projections.

I have always been open with the reality of where the Company is at. This emphasises and clarifies the reason for change (as in the Burning Platform), and allows greater visibility of your logic. As a standard, I would offer a series of options (if possible) and mention the decision criteria for change, emphasise where we are trying to get to and what we hope to achieve once there.

I have received kindness in response, for which I was pleasantly surprised. It demonstrates an appreciation that change is important and that they understand the need for me to take them on a journey, even if this results in job losses.

I tend to avoid making people redundant whenever possible as the message of negativity is harder to contain, although not impossible.

It is hard to contain the spread of negativity (you know where I am going with this). When change is seemingly unfounded, people cannot relate to any logic. The brain works overtime and projects that it will happen over and over, creating the feeling of insecurity, inertia and lack of motivation; all strongly linked to business failure.

So, it is similarly true then that a series of cuts or changes will exacerbate the problem, due to most people feeling like the cuts will continue until everyone is sacked!

It is therefore important that people understand your logic. If a series of steps are needed, outline these steps. If the next step depends on achieving a profit figure, for example, tell them, update them and let them understand your logic.

People will take two main views when it comes to communication, or shall we say, lack of:

1. No news is good news …
2. What are they not telling us?

In the first perspective, ignorance can be bliss, but it can also highlight a lack of interest. In the second perspective, interest is shown. This, in turn, may prompt insecurities one does not want initiated. For example, the loss of top performers due to insecurity, something all Leaders fear.

People's resilience when dealing with adverse change, particularly when they understand it, amazes me. I have been approached time and time again by people wanting a response, not for the obvious: 'is my job safe?' but rather, 'what more can I do to help?' – Wow.

Yes, help. How wonderful this concept is. And people offer to help. They have a vested interest in making this work, they want to come to work in the same place. Familiarity is a secure feeling. It's the reason many people go on holiday to the same destination. Everyone needs to create a feeling of security, for their own emotional wellbeing. We all need a bit of this from time to time (and a holiday or two, of course).

The other thing to mention here is staff involvement with upcoming changes.

If they understand the goals, listen to their ideas and suggestions for moving from A to B. You might be amazed.

Okay, I am back on the staff engagement trail again. Yes, so what? It is important.

Even if they have no ideas, crap ideas or just do not want to talk, engage them in the planning. Showing them the path and sharing your logic will resonate well in their brains. They will thank you for it. Your openness and the opportunity for them to contribute, is not something they will find in every Company.

A FEW REMINDERS

The role of the Leader can be a lonely place. Leaders are often caught up between politics, people and problems, often without a pat on the back or a well done, when they need it the most.

Decision-making sounds wonderful, of course. Although, with every decision, there is an impact on something or someone, making it impossible to be popular all the time.

So, why do we do it?

It makes a difference to people's lives. Though, corporate success can be hugely rewarding. Associating oneself with success is a good feeling and, hopefully, the overall rewards will justify the stressful long hours and never-ending stream of challenges that need resolving.

We have talked about Leadership, the kind that it is not about dictating, issuing instructions or pressing people to do something.

Okay, occasionally, when the building is on fire, a fireman will have no choice but to kick in the door and drag out the victims. In the business world, there are more sustainable models of engagement that can be used as an alternative, which I hope you have taken some comfort from.

Engaging your teams, setting goals and creating a journey plan will generate buy in, support and effective performance. The fears of providing too much information and increasing involvement will be outweighed by their support and assistance.

This involves communication, open communication. It's not enough to tell them what you think they need to hear. Openness goes a long way. Share your problems, share the success and share the rewards of the Company's success.

Set your goals and share them with your team. You need to ensure the goals can be realised in part at least as no one likes to be associated with failure all the time. Having longer term visions can be good if they do not replace key, realistic goals. The more outrageous and grand your dreams, the most inspiring it will be to many.

A strategy is a road map of how to get to the destination from where you are. Be clear and open about how someone's specific role impacts this journey and contributes to the success through their everyday actions.

People are amazing. Telling someone how to do everything will not give them the freedom they need to demonstrate how amazing they are. Many will just carry out your instructions to the best of their abilities.

Leading people must involve getting their input, their buy in and opinions on how to move from A to B. Not only will you receive some good ideas in return, you will also attract their appreciation. Asking for their input imparts a sense of importance.

It is also important to treat people as individuals. Few people think and react in the same way; each of them are special in their own way, as you are yourself.

Engaging people is not a box ticking exercise for a Corporate social responsibility package.

It is something you do because you believe that staff are the most important element for a business. Engaging a person shows that you care about them and their happiness. Their focus and journey translates into success for your business.

As a Leader, love your people, not your clients. Your people will return this emotion, so tailor responsibilities around the great skills they possess. Do not try and shoehorn them into a predestined job description, let the job description evolve around them. Create that culture of change.

Your talent pool is looking at you straight in the eye every day. What are you doing to develop, reward and incentivise them to do the best they can? If you do not talk to them regularly about this, other employers most certainly will.

As a Leader, you are not the most important person. You just play a different role. Do not try and pretend you are better than your team. Being different is the best you will ever achieve. Thinking you are better is far too subjective to confirm, thankfully.

Remember this when you find yourself caught up in the finer aspects one of your team could be doing. Ask yourself: why am I doing this? How does this help my colleague, my ability to be objective or my own career?

Work is a part of our lives, but it is not the only thing. Recognise why people go to work and ensure you create a culture that respects this.

Define who you are as a person. Do not compromise, stay tough and focused on the goal. Be careful not to be blinded by obstinacy, though.

Take advice, appoint advisers if you can; loneliness and isolation are killers. On the other hand, creating friendships with everyone can be an obstacle to objectivity.

Recognise the strengths in others. Let go of the minute detail and free your mind for objective thinking, planning, coaching and next actions.

Leave your team to deal with the here and now as often as you can. It's imperative you recognise when you need to manage and when you need to lead. Do not confuse the two and ensure you have time to step up.

Eliminate your weak links, they will destroy all hopes of a successful team, and drag you down into the abyss of despair.

Everyone wants to be part of a success story, otherwise why the hell would people go and work for peanuts at a large Global Company. So, create the journey and invite everyone to share, contribute and understand it.

Give people a focus and a voice. Let them use both to help you in your quest for betterment. Do not squash outspokenness and embrace feedback, however difficult it may be to hear.

Use your skills to show people the how and why. Help them get to a better place (skills wise, that is) from where they joined. That is the real definition of career progression. It's not just about getting a new title and salary increase.

When making changes, communicate and engage people. Do not make change after change without reasoning. You will lose trust, respect and create confusion and panic.

Money is not the key to engaging people. Although recognition, understanding and acknowledgment are helpful. Take time to look after your most precious asset – love your people, or another Company will.

The only way to give true empowerment to your team is to make yourself 'redundant'. This helps to make way for change, or you can use the space to generate next ideas, opportunities and growth.

Finally …

Is there a magic formula? The mix will vary depending on the Leader. Although, I can say for sure that there are several key ingredients, many of which I have discussed.

Remember how you became a Leader. You will have had successes to date, good results and the support of people who believed in your abilities.

None of this is by chance alone. You would not be where you are now if it weren't for others. Take a moment to reflect on how you need people to stay where you are. Never lose sight of their importance or their talents.

Your people are truly special. In my opinion, they are the key ingredient for your future success as a Leader.

Printed in Great Britain
by Amazon